THINKING ABOUT GOD

THINKING ABOUT GOD

Ruqaiyyah Waris Maqsood

American Trust Publications

To Waris Ali

Published by American Trust Publications
2622 East Main Street
Plainfield, Indiana 46168–2703

© American Trust Publications 1414/1994
All rights reserved. Published 1994

Library of Congress Cataloging in Publication Data
A catalog record for this book is available from the
Library of Congress

ISBN 0-89259-147-1

Printed in the United States of America

Cover design: Masood Athar

CONTENTS

FIRST, A FEW TRICKY QUESTIONS

> Righteousness is not to turn your faces toward the East or the West, but this is righteousness — to believe in God and the Last Day, and the angels, and the Book, and the messengers; to give one's wealth out of love for Him, for your family and for those without family,[1] the needy and the wayfarer, and those who ask (out of need) and for the freeing of slaves; and to be steadfast in prayer and to practice regular charity; and those who keep their promises when they promise (something), and the patient in pain (or suffering) and adversity, and throughout all periods of panic. Such are the people of truth, and those are the God-conscious (surah 2:177).

This is the statement of faith of a Muslim. There are no complicated theological involutions to go through, no necessity to have some kind of degree in esoteric knowledge. A simple soul can grasp it immediately.

So, what's the problem? Basically, it is this. A faith that is summed up so simply and directly has immediate and straight-forward appeal to the ordinary person, for no reason other than that it *is* simple and direct. The trouble is that today the majority of people are being educated to a level at which such a simple statement as this causes just a shade of embarrassment.

Are some of the concepts in it too simplistic? This is the Age of Science, and in the West it is still the Age of Atheistic Material-

---

[1]Literally, 'for relatives and orphans.'

ism, even though at long last scientists are beginning to admit publicly that they will have to go back to the 'drawing board,' because so many annoying spiritual 'facts' that upset materialistic theories have refused to go away, and consequently it is now no longer possible to ignore them and still call oneself a scientist.

God? Maybe He *does* exist. After all, some great Force was needed to make the Big Bang go bang in the first place, and who put into 'infinite space' the original ingredients of whatever it was that 'banged'?

Okay, let's say we can still keep God as some kind of a Force 'out there'—but angels? Messengers? Holy Books that consist of revealed messages from this supposed Original Energy Source? Come, come, now! Does that really still make sense, after all that scientists have taught us, and after rational humanity has managed to weed out all superstitious and primitive theological mumbo-jumbo?

Well, does it? To a Muslim, the answer is a resounding 'Yes!' Most Muslims wouldn't stop to think about it for a moment. The awareness of the existence of God has grown up with them from childhood. If they were born into observant families, the name of God was one of the first words they heard, and they would have been trained by conscientious parents to be aware of God in everything they do. The remembrance of God has become automatic for them, a part of their routine, as natural as breathing.

That's for the lucky ones. But apart from such convinced Muslims or convinced people of any other faith, in every society, no matter how scientific or rationalistic it may be, there are still countless thousands of people who feel a need in the depths of their souls to believe in God, yet nonetheless find that they cannot do so because they do not have reasonable answers to certain basic questions.

For example, if God exists, why can't anyone see Him? This is not intended as any disrespect or an affront; it is surely a fair question, if He really is 'there'. Why doesn't He show Himself and *prove* that He exists once and for all? Then everyone would realize how foolish they'd been in rejecting Him, and they would repent of their sins and wicked ways and turn to Him in worship, and the world would go on as it should.

Another thing—why is it that innocent people get hurt or catch painful diseases if it's true that God loves people? Why does

He allow people to starve to death, or drown in disastrous floods, or be buried by earthquakes or smothered by volcanic eruptions? Why does He allow accidents to happen, or terrible wars? Surely all these catastrophes simply prove that either God doesn't exist at all, or, if He does, He must be pretty impotent not to save people from all these disasters.

In any case, He can't be very kind. *We* wouldn't torture people like that, especially not people whom we know love and care about us. Therefore, one may conclude, He can't really be as kind as we are, unless He's just plain helpless to do anything about it all—in which case, why are we supposed to worship Him? It doesn't make much sense.

And what about all the things science has taught us? Did God *really* create the universe, or did it just come about by chance? Did God have anything to do with creating *us,* or could we just as well have been produced in a test tube? Do we really have a soul inside us, or are we no more than merely a collection of atoms? Can we really go on living after the death of our bodies, when we know they just rot away in the ground or are consumed by fire? Are there *really* such places as Paradise and Hell, and if there are, how can we reach the one and avoid the other?

All these questions are very important, and yet they are often ignored because the answers seem difficult to arrive at. So many people give up trying to find the answers even before they start, assuming that the whole business is just too complicated for their minds and that the simplest thing is to forget about it all, or otherwise to settle for believing the wise words of some teacher whose pronouncements have caught their interest. Others seem to think that science has proved all religion to be wrong, so it's quite all right to either ignore it or laugh at it.

But the believer has a different perspective. And since this book is about the Muslim perspective, we will look further at how a Muslim sorts out and deals with all these weighty and significant questions.

The Muslim believes in his or her heart that there *are* answers — true and correct ones. People who are 'born Muslims' have grown up with a particular world-outlook and life-view based on the teachings of the Qur'an, the collection of messages revealed over a period of more than twenty years to the prophet Muhammad, who was a direct descendant of the prophet Abraham through Abraham's son Ismael.

Seekers after truth who come into Islam from some other faith often do so with an immense feeling of relief: they have always wanted and tried to believe in God and to serve Him correctly, but were discouraged by doctrines and practices in their previous faiths which left them feeling uncomfortable, things which they could not rationally accept. Any such converts to Islam always claim that, to them, the beauty of Islam is that it is so rational. Indeed, many of them would not have become converts at all if they had found some aspects of the faith that did *not* appear rational. Hence before they embrace it, Islam is submitted to truly stringent criteria by these people.

In this day and age, when religion is under constant attack and is often regarded as old-fashioned superstition that should really be done away with by any intelligent and educated person, it seems necessary to arm believers with a little knowledge and a rational examination of certain suppositions concerning the existence of God, so that they can both think through their position more thoroughly for themselves and also acquire the ability to answer sensibly the accusations and questions of those who seek to attack their belief.

A closed, gullible mind is ill-equipped to cope with such questions, just as a closed, cynical one is. Some of the ideas that were laughed at by scientists only yesterday are now taken very seriously—fascinating ideas, some important and some just downright odd and interesting. That solid, dependable stuff of life that we have known as 'matter' has suddenly become a complete mystery once again; scientists are no longer convinced that it is either solid or dependable.

A definition of a believer as someone who 'accepts by faith what he knows in his heart cannot be true' is really the definition of a fool. If God exists and if He gave us intelligence, presumably He would like us to use it. The know-it-all, conceited veneer of some adults will have to go; the shallow hypocrisy, the selfishness, the laziness, the refusal to listen to others—all these must be set aside and replaced with the open, inquiring mind, an attitude of trust that there *are* answers to be found, and the sheer joy of discovery.

No amount of gimmickry will make a person believe in God. The answer does not lie in communal activities, clubs, or trying to latch on to whatever is popular among an in-group at any particular time. No person can justifiably be asked to believe in anything unless it seems reasonable to do so because of some personal insight which he or she has experienced.

Ask any average child to do anything and he or she will, in all probability, immediately and sensibly think, 'Why should I?' even if he or she is not impolite enough to voice the question. And such a question is actually quite reasonable. A person cannot justifiably be asked to believe anything in terms of a religion unless it seems reasonable.

The old questions our forefathers used to ask about religion remain just as valid today, or perhaps even more so, for this is an age that demands some kind of proof for everything. Defensive arguments meet with nothing but contempt. So let's go on the attack. Let's make, as our primary statement, the suggestion that perhaps, if a little more knowledge were given out first to someone who was going to criticize a belief in God, a lot of the grounds for the criticism would be cut out from under his feet.

Let's get down to it and have a real think about God. Why *do* believers, and specifically Muslims, believe the things they do?

CHAPTER TWO

DOES GOD EXIST?

Well, is there a God out there or isn't there? That has to be the one question of faith that really counts—because if there isn't, you can probably forget the rest.

Despite the millions of gallons of ink that have been spilled arguing over this question, it really is a blindingly simple choice. The choice is only one of two: either there is or there isn't. If there isn't, you can forget all the stuff about life after death, rewards and punishments for the way you live your life, the quaint notion that somewhere inside your brain is a thing called a conscience that tells you what you ought to do.

If there isn't a God, that's all just wishful thinking, or a crude attempt by some people in authority to make others do what they want. On the other hand, if there is a God, you have to face up to the whole business. Obviously, you shouldn't expect to be able to grasp it all in five minutes; you know perfectly well that wise people have grappled with problems of theology all their lives and still admit that they don't know all the answers.

Some people seem to believe all sorts of clap-trap that you know perfectly well goes completely against what scientists have discovered about the universe. Others have done a reasonable job of reconciling scientific discovery with their belief in God, but it remains a pretty hard job for many to sort out what's reasonable and what's just superstition.

In fact, it seems as if God has quite deliberately placed us in a neat little 'catch twenty-two' position. God's catch twenty-two is that He's created a universe full of things that we have no knowledge of and that it will always be impossible for us to understand

fully, and that He's so far above and beyond our sphere of understanding and experience that even the greatest brains in the world
can never fully understand Him. Let's look, for a moment, at how
the Muslim holy book, the Qur'an, puts it:

> No vision can grasp Him, but He grasps all vision; and
> He is above all comprehension and knows all things
> (surah 6:103).

> There is no God but He, the Living, the Eternal....And
> they cannot grasp anything of His knowledge except as He
> wills (surah 2:225).

Some may ask, but why should we believe in God at all? There
are actually lots of good reasons.

For one, we cannot just ignore and forget all about God.
There is something within ourselves that keeps nagging at us to
find the answer to this question. As rational beings we need to
understand life and the universe around us. How did it come
about? Who created it? Where does this order, harmony, beauty
and symmetry and balance come from? What lies behind the
forces of nature, against which we feel so insignificant and helpless? Who created them or how did they come to exist? We need
an answer, an explanation for this wondrous world we are put in.
There's scarcely a society in the history of the world that has not
grappled with these questions.

What couple, from the beginning of time, hasn't marveled at
the exquisite perfection of their new-born child, wondered at the
seeming miracle of its creation, and dearly hoped, or prayed, that
destiny or their 'god' would keep it safe?

Modern scientific discoveries have made us even more aware
of the exquisitely structured universe we are a part of. Now we are
in a better position to appreciate the amazing design and function
of our minds and bodies, and yet we are helpless as ever against
the powers of nature; we are unable to control our own fate, let
alone the workings of nature. Each movement of far away millions
of galaxies and myriads of constellations of stars affects our existence on earth, yet we have no control over them. We are placed
at a distance from the center of our solar family — the sun —
which is crucial in terms of our survival, but we have no control or

say in the matter. How utterly dependent we are, how privileged and yet how helpless! And the most fascinating thing is that despite our helplessness and dependence, we have got the best of the deal. Our own physical bodies, eyes, ears, and faculty of thinking are wonderful gifts. How do we explain this dependence and this privileged position of ours in this world? Without believing in a God, All-Powerful and yet All-Merciful, can this question be resolved?

Belief in God seems to be a part of our natural disposition. And in our hours of desperate need, we *still* reach out to the idea of a god, someone who cares and is there to help us when all seems hopeless. There seems to be something in our human nature that *wants to believe* in a personal God who intimately knows us, actually cares about us, and has the power to help us. All of us, no matter what name we give ourselves — atheists or otherwise —are in this sense, as it were, natural believers. This idea that we have a God is so deeply rooted in our hearts and minds that if we cannot come up with a rational answer, we go and invent our 'gods'. That explains why man is restless until he finds his True God, 'For without doubt in the remembrance of God do hearts find satisfaction' (surah 13:28).

Now if there is a God, all indications are that He is Sublime and Perfect. To be perfect means God must be perfectly just. But looking at His handiwork, this world, we discover with a shock that it is far from being perfect. More often than not, crooks, murderers, smart but dishonest folks seem to have 'success,' prosperity, and to enjoy and wield power, while poor, honest, just men and women are deprived of the rewards of their labor. Here the great benefactors of mankind, like Jesus, are spurned, while evil men, dictators, and enemies of man and God flourish and enjoy power and prestige. Where is the justice in all this? This is evidently a very incomplete world; there must therefore be another world where God's justice shall manifest itself fully and perfectly. A belief in a Kind, Merciful, and Just God naturally leads us to believe in a life after life, where men and women shall be fully rewarded. In other words, there must be a Day of Reckoning, for otherwise it would mean that good and evil are equal. Human nature abhors such a suggestion. A voice within us tells us this cannot be true, and we believe it and in this life treat others accordingly; we do differentiate between the good and the bad, even though they be closely related to us, our own children. We like the one and are displeased with the other. The Qur'an supports this testimony of human nature and tells us that indeed 'the blind and the seeing are not alike; nor are the depths of darkness and the light; nor are the (chilly) shade and the (radiant) heat of the sun: nor alike are those that are living and those that are dead (surah 35:19-22), nor are the good and the bad equal (surah 68:35). 'The people of the fire and the people of the garden are not equal; only the people of the Garden will achieve (ultimate) happiness' (surah 59:20).

The Day of Judgement is at once an expression of God's grace and His justice. If He is merciful, He must also be just, for otherwise that would mean cruelty and wrong to the victims and the oppressed ones, and a license to the evil to indulge and exult in their corruption and iniquity.

Now if there *is* such a thing as a Day of Judgement and a time when people will be rewarded or punished for the way they've lived their lives, then obviously God wouldn't be at all fair if He hadn't let people know what they were supposed to be doing before they did it. He could never blame you for not doing what He wants you to do if He hadn't told you what He wanted. To do so would be blatant injustice rather than perfect justice.

Therefore, it stands to reason that if God exists, He must have revealed *something* about Himself for human beings to reflect on and understand, some kind of 'rule of life' for people to follow. All religions, especially Islam, insist on God's relationship with ourselves. Since God is perfectly fair, He has sent revelations to human beings of every single generation. There have always been people of special insight who were able to 'see' or grasp a good deal more about God than others, and they understood it as their responsibility to inform everyone else about what God wanted or expected them to do.

God has never actually forced people to do anything—except, I suppose, you could say He 'forced' these special people to be 'revealers' or 'messengers'. At least, once they had grasped the nature of their insight, they were never able to put the matter aside. It took over their entire lives, as well as influencing thousands of other people to accept what they taught.

Well, you might say, what about *your* generation? Where is the special prophet telling *you* what to do? There seem to be so many different religions, and they all insist they are right and the others are wrong. Who is supposed to give you the truth? Can God really blame you if you can't make up your mind, or if you finally decide that they are all as good as one another so that it doesn't matter which one you choose, or decide that none of them really matters at all as long as you do your best?

If you've arrived at the stage of reasoning at which you're questioning things and searching through the darkness for something that can make sense out of existence, then perhaps the time has come for you to sit down and try to work out what you believe.

Human beings are like ants, running around in the garden. Busy little creatures, totally occupied with their chores and comings and goings, completely unaware of the All-Seeing Eyes of the Eternal Watcher until such a moment as He chooses to stop us in our tracks and make us see.

Over the centuries, there seems to have been a chain of awareness relating to the existence of God, different generations being granted such awareness through various enlightened people whom God brought close to Himself. These chosen people — known as prophets — called people to God and organized those who responded to their call into communities of faith.

The three great monotheist religions are, as we know, Judaism, Christianity and Islam. Of these, Islam differs somewhat from the other two, in that it claims to be the final and summative statement of genuine revealed knowledge of God, encompassing all the truths taught by the messengers of God who lived prior to the prophet Muhammad, and remains eternally valid due to the very nature of its miraculous revelation in the form of exact-word statements that were learned, written down and passed on to all future generations.

All religion starts with realization. It lies at the very heart of religion, and it can begin even when faith, or even the possibility of faith, is very weak. No religious leader or teacher in the world can *make* it happen, although they may do their best to guide people toward God.

One of the most important declarations which Muslims believe to have been made by God is that 'Truth stands out clear from error' (surah 2:256). If a thing is true, it doesn't matter what anyone thinks or says about it, it will in the end be self-evident, and people, when they attain reason, will either come to realize it or deliberately choose to ignore it.

You cannot be *forced* to feel faith any more than you can be forced to feel love. It's a matter of awareness. 'It is impossible to impose a belief by means of decree, terror, pressure, violence or force. Every pedagogue can give a number of examples of how children resist persistent guidance in one direction and how they can consequently develop an interest in completely opposite behavior ... Man cannot be drilled like an animal.'[2] One minute there may be nothing there at all; you're ambling along your way, whistling nonchalantly, the sky is blue, the birds are singing — then—wham! The whole universe suddenly changes, and you become the most insightful and enlightened being anywhere around because of your flash of insight, yet at the same time you realize you are the most insignificant speck of dust.

You suddenly become aware of His Presence, and—well, you don't know how to describe it.

You want to crumble into dust in the face of this intense and searing knowledge that you've never experienced before, and you feel the most incredible wave of feeling that you can't explain, something moving in the depth of your heart, a kind of over-whelming joy and gratitude and amazement that God sees and actually cares about you. Not only that, He sees everything you go through and He loves you. Now, all at once, you can see that even at those times when you felt most alone, you weren't alone at all, since God was with you. You've heard about people suddenly breaking down and bursting into tears and have probably thought how ridiculous that was, but now, all at once, you want to sing and cry at the same time.

This, actually, is nothing new. The acute realization that *God knows you* is one that has brought even the toughest people in every generation to their knees. And now, all of a sudden, it's your turn! This is a common experience of all true believers, including Muslims. The word 'Muslim' means 'one who submits,' a person who makes a conscious decision to put his or her will sec-ond to God's, insofar as they can understand God's will through the words of the Qur'an, or through indications which come through the events of their lives. It is in this sense that Islam rec-ognizes as Muslims all devout people who were submitted to God

---

[2]*Islam Between East and West*, Alija Ali Izetbegovic, American Trust Publications, 1993, p. 114.

and lived anywhere or at any period of history before the time of the Prophet Muhammad. Indeed, the Qur'an states that all prophets of God, such as Abraham, Moses and Jesus, brought the same message: Islam; and their true followers were all 'Muslims.'

A Muslim, God forbid, is not someone who worships Muhammad! This is absolute nonsense, even though Muslims love Muhammad and cherish the stories about him and study his sayings and way of life. The Qur'an itself makes it completely clear that worship of a prophet, or any other human being whomsoever, as if he were God, or part of God, is such a blatant misunderstanding of the exalted and unique nature of God that the worshipper has completely missed the understanding of what God is. In the words of the Qur'an:

> God is the One who created you, then provided your sustenance, then will cause you to die, (and) then will give you life again. Are there among your 'partners' any who can do any of these things? Glorified and exalted is He above any 'partners' they ascribe to Him (surah 30:40).

> Behold! Truly whatever is in the heavens and on earth belongs to God. And those who call upon others than God follow nothing but suppositions, and do nothing but (follow) guesswork (surah 10:66).

To believe that God has 'partners' who share His powers and exalted status or that He is somehow made up of separate aspects or entities is what Islam calls '*shirk*,' an Arabic word pronounced 'sheerk,' which means to divide the nature of God or give others shares of His Godhood. Muslims maintain that this is the error committed by Christians, who, out of intense piety and devotion and genuine love of God, misunderstood the true compassion of the One God and elevated prophet Jesus to the status of God.

An integral part of the Muslim statement of faith is that Muhammad is a *prophet* of God. What does this mean? It means that around two thousand years after the prophet Moses and six hundred years or so after the prophet Jesus, another man was called and set apart by God to reveal His Message. As God willed, this man was an Arab of the Quraish tribe, a descendant of the prophet Abraham, born in Makkah, a city in Arabia. In fact, this second part of the Muslim statement is an essential part of faith, and the one which makes Muslims different from any other believers in God. Because they believe that the message which Muhammad brought was the absolute, unadulterated word of Almighty God, in which God Himself unequivocally declares Muhammad to be His prophet, Muslims affirm their belief in the genuine prophetic calling of Muhammad, and that the message revealed through him was the final, complete and ultimate revelation of God's guidance to humanity.

This brings us to the third item of faith for a Muslim, one that is the cause of the whole business. The revealed message that the Blessed Muhammad heard and passed on is available for us to read and study for ourselves, the Holy Qur'an. As the revealed message of God, the Muslims take it as guide in their individual and social lives, even if at times they may not fully comprehend it or parts of it may not suit the desires of some people.

All Muslims have to face up to these three challenges of faith: First, do they truly and genuinely believe in their hearts that God exists and is aware of them, and knows everything that they do and think? Second, do they really believe that Muhammad is God's true prophet, and since it is asserted as part of the revelation, that he is the *last* prophet? Third, do they really believe that the Qur'an consists of God's direct messages, revealed to Muhammad in order that he would convey them to all humanity as a means of showing people how to lead clean and virtuous lives, to warrant eternal reward and avoid damnation for disobedience? A person who accepts Islam enters into a sort of a covenant to follow the teachings of the Blessed Prophet Muhammad and the revealed words of God, the Qur'an, concerning which God Himself says:

> This is the revelation of the Book in which there is no doubt, from the Lord of the Worlds. Do they say, 'He has forged it?' No, it is the Truth from your Lord, that you may guide a people to whom no warner had come before you, in order that they might receive guidance (surah 32:1-2).

Actually, the statement of faith of a Muslim is extremely simple. It is this:

La ilaha illal Lahu wa Muhammadur Rasulullah (There is no God but Allah,[3] and Muhammad is the Prophet of God.) In other words, it is an acknowledgement that God exists and that the Blessed Muhammad, who lived over fourteen hundred years ago, is *the* last prophet, and hence the prophet for all of mankind for all time to come.

But, you may ask, what does this have to do with people who are not Muslim, or who aren't sure that they believe in *any* scripture at all? What of those who aren't even sure of God's existence? Is there any evidence of His existence other than the plain assertions of religious scriptures or the emotion-filled claims of convinced believers and theologians?

After all, a person is perfectly justified in maintaining a degree of skepticism, unless that is taken too far, resulting in a refusal to maintain an open mind and an unwillingness to seriously examine what is presented as evidence. In a matter of such significance, it surely seems better for us to try to maintain an open mind when thinking about God. So let us go on and have a look at it, and consider if there is any further evidence.

---

[3]*Allah* means 'God' in Arabic and is considered by Muslims to be His proper name.

CHAPTER THREE

IS SEEING BELIEVING?

Surely, if God would only make some kind of public appearance in the sky so that everyone could see Him, then we would all know for certain that He exists and believe in Him. Or would we? It sounds a good idea, but still there are catches!

The trouble with human beings is that they have become too clever for their own good. They think they know everything. The advances made in technology during this century have been so brilliant that everyone knows how to use electricity and electronics, operate machines, use computers, and so on. Very few of us, of course, know how to make these things, but being able to use them has become such a part of our everyday lives that we almost have a sense that credit for them belongs to us.

Human beings play around in space and carry out technological operations in weightless conditions hundreds of miles above the surface of our planet. There hardly seems to be anything that humans cannot do once they put their minds to it. And yet, they really are incredibly ignorant about almost everything.

Take this world of ours, the one we think we know so well. The first question we might ask is 'How do we know it is really there at all?' And what about our own selves: 'Are *we* really real?' Does that sound crazy? It isn't really. We seem to have an entirely different existence while we're asleep. So how are we to decide which is the *real* world—the one we experience when we are awake, or the one when we are asleep? Which is reality? In fact, how can we figure out whether we're awake or asleep now, at this very moment? You may think you're awake, but it could all be a dream, couldn't it? It's no good pinching yourself; that could be part of the dream too.

In any case, if you are making the assumption that you must be awake because you are reading this book, that still doesn't answer the question of which of our lives is the real one. Maybe our true state is the one we're in when we put our bodies to bed, and what we're doing now is simply spending a few hours awake in order to stoke them up with food and evacuate waste products so that we can get on with being asleep again.

And what about the things around us? Are *they* real? When we examine them closely, they certainly seem to be — solid objects like tables and chairs and so forth. But philosophers will tell you there is quite a game involved when you try to define what a table actually is.

You can see the thing in front of you. There it is — there's no doubt about it. If you kick it, it will hurt your foot. You can balance your plate upon it and safely eat your meal. You can even dance on it if you wish. No, surely there can be no doubt that the table exists and it's a pretty solid object.

But what would happen if you chipped a piece off it and put it under a powerful microscope? The whole concept would then become completely different. Your table would no longer seem solid and still, but a wriggling mass of little unidentified bits and pieces. So, incidently, would your finger, or the plate, or the meal upon it.

So, which is the *real* table? The one you see with your own eyes, or the one the microscope sees? Obviously our eyes see a much more limited table than the microscopic view provides. Doesn't this suggest that we see *everything* in a limited fashion? If we could see as the microscope sees, we would never actually see the table at all, for it would become a complex object far too vast for us to comprehend.

In fact, when we think about it, we have to consider the limits of our vision to be a mercy. If we could see everything the microscope sees, we would never want to eat or drink anything unless we could get used to the idea that a drop of water was seething with wriggling life forms. As another example, you have only to stand in a shaft of strong sunlight to reconsider the whole phenomenon of breathing. It's hard to believe that all those particles of dust are going in and out of our nostrils and lungs, not to mention all those revolting microbes crawling about in and out of our eyes or on the top layer of our skins!

The point of all this is that our eyes don't really tell us very much about the reality of our world at all. What we see is very limited (although it suits us to have it this way) and somewhat misleading.

Here's another strange example. We think we're seeing people and things the right way up, but in fact the images on our retinas are inverted and we see everything upside down. You don't believe this? Check it out with a scientist. You think you know what you look like? Not at all; you can only see yourself in a mirror. And if you want to know what distortion *that* gives, try the simple experiment of holding up some writing to the mirror and reading it. Got it? You are also seeing *yourself* in reverse!

Not only that, but although you may think you know what colors are, this again is only a subjective experience. You have no way of telling that what you call green and what somebody else calls green are the same thing. In point of fact, the world isn't in color at all. What we think of as colors are simply the different ways in which our eyes interpret different wave-lengths of light bouncing off things.

Rubbish? Look at the sky. Okay, it's blue. But where does it start being blue? The air around you is obviously colorless, and it's still colorless outside the window. There's no fixed point at which it suddenly becomes blue. You could go up in a plane or in a spacecraft, and you'd never come across place where the air suddenly took on its lovely summer-sky shade. It is all an illusion, a trick of nature, an interpretation of our sensory apparatus.

To conclude our little ramble into the realm of sight — if our sense of sight is so unreliable, then how can we really find out anything about our world, let alone about God?

What about our other senses? We're supposed to have five — sight, hearing, smell, touch and taste. We generally use these senses to find out whether or not a thing is there. Unfortunately, the same principles apply as above; all our senses are limited. It's a well-known fact that some animals have far better developed senses than ours; for example, a dog can track down a person or missing object simply by its smell. The police sometimes use whistles that have a range too high for a criminal's ear but which dogs are able to hear.

We wouldn't last long in a jungle, if we happened to be dropped in one, if it weren't for one redeeming factor: the human brain. By means of it, we've worked out clever ways to make up for our natural deficiencies. Slow-moving, puny and defenseless our bodies may be, yet we are still kings of the animal kingdom. All animal and plant life seems to exist for our benefit. But does it actually? We're so blind that we often don't realize that from another point of view we may be seen as simply the food supply for the world of microbes. Germs just eat us and then cast us aside!

So, if our senses don't tell us very much about our own world, why should we expect them to tell us anything at all about *God?* Later, we will consider the possibility that what I can see of myself isn't even really *me*, but just my collection of atoms. Now if I can't see my own real self, even though I know I exist, likewise it may well be that God does exist but we cannot see Him!

Obviously, God isn't limited to any form and isn't floating around somewhere in space. God is part of the realm of the unknown and unseen; His presence signifies Intelligence, Love, Power, and none of these things can be seen with the human eye. We know these qualities or attributes have real existence because we can observe their effects, but the actual reality of them no one can see.

CHAPTER FOUR

SOUND SENSE

The whole business about seeing God was all rather complicated. In any case, it is commonly accepted among the devout that God is unseeable anyway, beyond our vision and comprehension, even if we knew what we were looking for, or even if our eyes constituted equipment that was suitable for the task, which they patently are not in their present form.

This idea of the unseeable nature of God goes back to the earliest of traditions, even when expressed in anthropomorphic language. The Prophet Moses, for example, is reported to have specifically asked to see God's glory manifested (Exodus 33:20), and was told that 'you cannot see My face, for humans cannot see Me and live'. This story goes on to speak of how Moses took shelter in the cleft of a rock and was covered with God's hand while God passed by; then, when God took away His hand, says the Bible, Moses was invited to look upon His back, for he would never be able to see God's face.

Was this supposed to be a genuine incident involving a sighting of God by one of His more famous followers, or was the whole incident made up? Was what was seen God Himself, or something else? However one interprets this ancient story, there is no doubt that its main teaching is that God is beyond the perception of human beings in this life. The presence of God is so sublime, so searing in its purity and power, that no human can withstand its force. The Qur'an refers to a similar incident and says:

When his Lord revealed His glory on the mount, He made it (the mountain) as dust, and Moses fell down in a swoon. When he recovered his senses he said: 'Glory to You! To You I turn in repentance, and I am the first to believe' (Qur'an 7:143).

Is there any other scriptural evidence to support this phenomenon? Well, throughout the Old Testament, God is said to have protected those with whom He wished to commune by surrounding Himself with a protective cloud, the *Shakinah* (Leviticus 16:2). At Mount Sinai, when He gave the Law to Israel, 'the appearance of the glory of the Lord was like a devouring fire...and the people could see it' (Exodus 24:17). A dark cloud covered the mountain, and out of this cloud came lightnings and thunder, the blare of a trumpet and a loud voice (Exodus 19:16-19; 24:15; Hebrews 12:18,19).

Moses is said to have pitched a 'tent of meeting' in which he communed with God: 'When he entered the tent, the pillar of cloud would descend and stand at the door of the tent and the Lord would speak with Moses. When the people saw this pillar they would rise up and worship. Thus the Lord would speak to Moses face to face, as a man speaks to his friend' (Exodus 33:9-11). When Moses came down from Sinai, says the Bible, the experience had actually affected the skin of his face, which now shone, and he was obliged to wear a veil (Exodus 34:29,33).

When the tabernacle was set up, a cloud resided over it, and 'God's glory filled the tabernacle' to the extent that Moses was unable to enter (Exodus 40:34-35; compare I Kings 8:10-12; Revelation 15:8). According to the Bible, the Israelites could apparently see the cloud quite plainly; when it rose, they prepared to break camp, and when it moved, they followed its direction to the next camp. After the building of the temple, a brilliant cloud protected the Ark of the Covenant from human eyes. The high priest was allowed to enter the temple only annually, on the Day of Atonement; at other times, he and other priests were said to have been protected from God's Presence by a curtain the thickness of a man's fist.

In the New Testament, the cloud was still in evidence. On the one occasion when a group of disciples was said to have heard what purported to be God's Voice, it was described as coming from a very bright cloud which overshadowed Jesus on the Mount of Transfiguration (Matthew 17:5). When Jesus ascended into

Heaven, 'a cloud caught him up from their vision' (Acts 1:9), and he predicted that when he returned to earth, people would 'see the Son of Man coming in a cloud with great power and glory' (Luke 21:27; Matthew 24:30; Mark 13:26; Revelation 14:14).

The cloud presumably represented the invisible presence of God, observers being expected to 'see' the meaning with their 'spiritual eye'. The kind of seeing Jesus spoke of was spiritual: 'For judgement I came into this world that those who do not see may see' (John 9:39).

Now, there is all the difference in the world between seeing a bright cloud, or anything else that represents the presence of God, and seeing God Himself. It was said to have been not God Himself, but God's messenger, an angel within the cloud, that led the tribes of Israel through the wilderness (Exodus 23:20-21; 33:2; Isaiah 63:9).

The New Testament teachings of Jesus concerning the impossibility of a human being's ever being able to see God is similar to that of the earlier prophets. In John 6:46, Jesus is supposed to have said: 'No man can see the Father; except him who is from God: he has seen the Father'. The prologue to the Gospel, however, states the matter rather differently: 'No one has ever seen God; the only Son who is in the bosom of the Father, he has made Him known'(John 1:18). St. John's Epistle is clearer: 'No person has ever seen God; but if we love one another, God abides in us and His love is perfected in us' (I John 4:12).

Now, according to the Islamic understanding, the revelations of the Qur'an came to the prophet Muhammad through the angel Gabriel, the messenger of God. On the occasion of the Prophet's ascent into Paradise, the event known as *Lailat al-Mi'raj* (the Night of the Ascent), Muhammad was shown Heaven and Hell and their inhabitants; but although he is said to have drawn nearer to God than any other human being, he was nevertheless not allowed (or perhaps we should say 'was not able') to *see* God or to pierce the mystery of God's Being. There was a barrier that could not be crossed, even by the angel Gabriel. The Bright Cloud of Unknowing prevented his eyes—whether in his elevated physical or spiritual body, or in vision or trance, however one interprets the Ascent he made—from witnessing the Ineffable Almighty.

Hence any further considerations about seeing God with our eyes end up in a blind alley. But what about our sense of hearing?

Well, for a start, if we are just thinking about messages transmitted through conventional sound, let's consider the possibility that, just as our seeing equipment is very limited, our sound-receiving gear is equally limited, so that even if God were transmitting, we would not, in our present state, be able to 'pick Him up'.

Our ears are, in any case, extremely limited in what they hear. If you were blind and couldn't use your eyes at all, you'd probably have an extra-sensitive sense of hearing. And if you shut your eyes now and just sit and listen, you'll probably be amazed at all the different things you can hear that you'd normally ignore.

Remember that our ears are not nearly as efficient as those of many animals. We've already commented on police dogs responding to whistles whose sounds are too high-pitched for the human range of hearing. There are subsonic sounds, too, and scientists say that it would be possible to develop a gun that could flatten everything, just by using sound waves we can't even hear.

But all this talk of sound and hearing sound is really only another of the odd illusions of the universe in which we live. Strangely enough, the 'noisy' environment we inhabit is actually totally silent, and what we think of as sound is again just a matter of waves, as much an illusion as color.

Sight and sound—these two aspects of 'reality' are real mind-benders. We should thank God, if we acknowledge Him at all, for two things: first, that He has granted us these two illusions that we always think of as being real, because otherwise we'd have to pass our lives like the blind and deaf, and second, that He set limits on what we could perceive, so that we are not driven crazy by the whizzing haze of atomic entities or the cacophony of all the world's noises blasting at us unprotected!

What we call sound is actually a system of moving waves which are picked up by the delicate mechanism of our ears. These waves are vibrations; when they travel down the ear, they hit the eardrum and make it vibrate also, and these vibrations are then carried to the inner ear by a series of small bones. The inner ear is filled with liquid, and the vibrations travel through it to the nerves and from there to the brain. Finally, the brain sorts out the meaning of the vibrations picked up and interprets them as sounds. Without the brain to interpret the vibrations, the sounds would simply not exist. If any part of the equipment needed on the journey of these vibrations were faulty, the 'sounds' would come out all wrong.

If you still think you're really making noises and not just emitting vibrations, try to think of how the telephone works—all those people talking at once, all those wires, all those miles of distance crossed. Your words don't travel at all, just the vibrations. The telephone changes mechanical vibrations into electrical, and back again. The important element of the concept of sound is actually the receiver. The vibrations come to absolutely nothing if there is no receiver to give them meaning.

You may have heard of the Zen Buddhist 'koan' or riddle about what sort of sound is made by a tree falling in the depths of an uninhabited jungle. If you think about it carefully, you'll see the problem; it all depends on what you mean by 'sound.' Think about it. If sound is really only the vibrations picked up by someone's eardrums, and if no one's eardrums are there to pick them up, did the sound ever exist? Can a sound exist without an ear to hear it?

Possibly God *is* speaking to us, but either our ears are not sensitive or receptive enough to pick up the vibrations, or our brains are not developed enough to make sense of the vibrations they receive. In other words, God has not chosen to communicate with us through air waves—our ears, otherwise He would have enabled us all to decipher these sound vibrations. Or perhaps any other type of apparatus we may have been given for the purpose isn't receiving; maybe we just aren't 'tuned in'. After all, the room you're sitting in at the moment is full of radio waves, but unless you have some receiving equipment—what we used to call a 'wireless set'—you won't be able to hear them at all. And here, once again, we have to thank God, assuming that He exists, for His merciful limitation of our senses.

But what about the prophet Muhammad, or, for that matter, all the other prophets of old who claimed that they could hear the Voice of God? Not only the Qur'an, but also the Christian and Jewish holy books, are full of reports of individuals who claimed to be hearing this Voice. The usual prophetic introductory remark is, 'Thus saith the Lord'. What were they hearing — or are these stories simply untrue?

Well, if you read the passages carefully, they never actually state that the prophets were hearing the Voice of God with their ears. It is far more likely that they were picking up something transmitted directly to their minds or hearts by a power peculiar to God. We will never know. But we do know from scriptural references that those who reported having received communication from God did receive messages which others were incapable of hearing, and that those messages profoundly affected those who received them. For God, when He wants something to be known or understood, seems to work 'heart to heart' and makes His message not only known, but felt, leaving those who have 'heard' Him with no doubt that they have heard the voice of God.

Obviously the physical heart is no more than a pump, but its inner meaning is quite different. You do things 'with all your heart,' or you don't feel like something because 'your heart isn't in it'. The heart can 'melt' with sorrow or affection, or 'fail' as a symbol of losing courage, or 'break' out of grief. Unsympathetic people are 'hard-hearted'; others may be 'faint-hearted,' 'whole-hearted,' 'tender-hearted,' and so on.

Perhaps all emotions affect the non-physical heart, or maybe the heart itself, in forming the personality of its owner, affects the emotions. It has certainly become the organ that represents inner expression. Somehow the heart represents the inner depth of a person, and it seems to be to the heart that God speaks and on it that God's spirit acts.

The mind is the intellect or information-and-knowledge-gathering-center which thinks and reasons and comes to conclusions, but the heart at times overrules the judgements or conclusions of the mind. The mind may recommend one course of action, but if the heart has no desire to pursue that course and steadfastly refuses to do so, a person nearly always follows the heart and not the logical mind.

From the perspective of reflection, a person may present any outward appearance to the world that he or she chooses, but what counts with God is the state of that person's heart, and since God can see into the human heart, He judges accurately one's motivation and consequent worthiness or unworthiness. It is thus understood to be the operation of the spirit of God in the hearts of believers that motivates them to speak out, endure persecution or bear all sorts of trials and difficulties.

According to the Bible, Jeremiah once made a decision not to speak in God's name any longer, but said, 'In my heart God's word proved to be like a burning fire shut up in my bones; and I got tired of holding it in, and I was unable to endure it' (Jeremiah 20:9).

The Islamic concept of *qalb*, or heart, follows the same lines of thought. Whenever Prophet Muhammad heard the Angel Gabriel, it was not something that anyone else present with him could hear. It is stated in the Qur'an itself that it was sent down to the Prophet's heart.[4]

The traditions concerning the Blessed Muhammad's receiving revelations are varied. Sometimes, he said, he heard a voice directly, and sometimes he saw and heard the angel Gabriel. In each case, however, the Blessed Muhammad clearly and plainly *heard* the message that was conveyed to him by the angel.

But it was not hearing in the normal sense of the word, for those with him and around him on the occasions when he received the revelations could not hear what he was hearing. The 'voice' was an internal one; it was as if the Blessed Muhammad could hear with a faculty that other people did not possess. God did not boom out His messages for the entire world; they passed through the person and 'medium' of the Blessed Prophet.

History notes that the effect of these messages, both on the individual who received them and on the audiences to whom they were passed on, was astounding. No messages of God ever reached any human beings without amazing the ones who received them, altering their lives and firing them with inspiration for good— often at the cost of their own lives.

Sometimes those messages revealed sublime truths. At other times they were instructive about virtue and proper conduct in private and public life, and were practical, down-to-earth and often quite detailed. And sometimes the Voice revealed a complex message for the arrangement of human society and interaction.

But did God speak to Prophet Muhammad through the medium of ordinary sound? Obviously He did not. If a physical God were out in space and speaking, this would be traceable as a power source, and such a wonderful transmitter of energy would certainly have been pinpointed on our scientific equipment. We are picking up transmissions from quasi-stellar objects in the deepest

---

[4]'Verily, this is a revelation from the Lord of the Worlds: with it came down the Spirit of Faith and Truth — to your heart and mind, that you may admonish' (Qur'an 26:193).

reaches of space; therefore, if God were 'transmitting' in the traditional sense of the word, there is no doubt that we would all be able to pick up His messages.

If God were to speak to us using the medium of sound, and if it were assumed that He resided somewhere in far-off space, it would raise yet another mechanical problem: the fact that conventional sound takes a very long time to travel. Some of our jet planes now travel faster than sound, although sound doesn't travel anywhere near as fast as light, which takes eight minutes to reach the earth's surface from the sun, 93 million miles away. So if God spoke to us at any given moment, expressing Himself through the medium of our time-scale and wave-physics, the message probably wouldn't arrive until long after it was useful to us, and possibly not until after we were dead. Since God is God, He knows precisely how to get the message to us directly, at the exact moment He wishes it, without needing to use the medium of sound, as we know it, at all.

Einstein's theory of relativity helps to illustrate the problem. Time doesn't seem very relative to us because we are programmed to think in very small units and measures—our 'local' experience. But when you apply the theory to the stars and planets in space, it immediately reveals the impossibility of giving precise dates for anything. If the sun blew up, for example, we would see it, if we survived, eight minutes later, but people on more distant planets wouldn't know anything about it until the light waves eventually reached them, which would depend on the distance. It's a strange thought that the stars we see in the night sky, so far away from us, may not actually be there at all now; we are only seeing what *was* there hundreds of light years ago, which is the time it took the light from those stars to reach us. In order to get a 'sound' message to us, God would have to have spoken to us centuries before we were born. Does that make any kind of sense? Not really, when God has other, much more direct means of communicating with us.

Now that it is clear that God hasn't chosen to reveal Himself personally to each of us directly through the media of sight and sound, shouldn't we, instead of considering means related to 'outer space,' be focussing on our 'inner space'? Perhaps, instead of concentrating on attempting to find a physical means of perceiving Him, we should really start to use our non-physical attributes — our non-material receiving apparatus.

For example, isn't it true that God often 'speaks' to us through our consciences? And yet, who can possibly identify what a 'conscience' is? It isn't a physical thing at all; you can't extract it, lay it out on a dissecting table, and point out the conscience to the human eye. And yet it's there all right, as we've all experienced.

CHAPTER FIVE

A TOUCHY PROBLEM

No sooner do we really latch on to the problems involved if we have been thinking of God as the kind of Being whom we could see or hear, than we must begin to work out the fact that the whole business of imagining that God has a limited physical body is both inappropriate and far too naive.

It is often difficult to prevent youngsters from forming in their minds an image of God as some kind of venerable old man who lays down the law and watches over us. The Christian representations of God, for instance, often show him an aged white man with a long beard, wearing flimsy clothing.

This is more than just a cultural matter. It involves the whole matter of creating God in our own image—of making Him appear to be as we imagine Him, and then attempting to convince everyone else that our imaginings are the truth. This is obviously one of the prime dangers of thinking of God in human terms; for example, the word 'father' means so many different things to different people, depending on their experience of fathers. It can be no accident, surely, that many of the people who adhere to a belief in 'God-the-Father' have a limited view of His nature, regarding Him as a stern judge, always spotting our minutest failings, overseeing our most private and intimate moments and thoughts like a prying parent, most concerned that we never do anything in private of which we should be ashamed in public.[5]

---

[5]It is interesting that the Qur'an refers to God by ninety-nine Holy Names, which are actually His perfect attributes or characteristics. But, while God is frequently referred to in the Qur'an as *al-Rabb* (Lord), not once is He referred to as *Ab*, or Father.

Now, any religious person who maintains that God knows precisely what people are thinking and doing at any moment is bound to feel uncomfortable when he or she wants to do something which is sinful or regarded as sinful. This is obviously a useful curb on our wilder desires. But the notion of God as a strict, unbending, censorial figure is not the whole story by any means. People who have suffered from overbearing fathers who have been impossible to please, and of whom one as a child has generally walked in dread rather than affection, often end up with a fear-ridden, obsessive attitude toward the Almighty, which is disappointing as well as false, rooted as it is, in our limited personal experiences.

Service of God carried on in these terms is not the result of real faith and trust and love, but of fear; or, if one feels that one has managed to be successful in subordinating one's life completely to rituals that are supposed to give Him pleasure, is performed with a rather superior, smug self-satisfaction and the selfish desire to be patted on the back.

The human mind has a tendency to think of all reality as being tangible, because we live in a physical world. It may seem easier for us to conceive of a god that has a physical presence than one that does not. However, if we pause to consider the *apparent* reality of the things we can see and hear and touch, we may realize that the apparent reality of even the ordinary things in our everyday world isn't at all as we perceive and experience them to be. Let's just examine this a little. Surely we can't be wrong about whether a thing is solid or not. If you stub your toe on a brick, you certainly won't have any doubt about this question. And yet, if you place that brick under a microscope, it does seem to become a different thing. And so does your toe.

Everything in our known universe is just a series of combinations of the minute particles which we call atoms—everything, whether it's a table or your toe. These atoms are very difficult things to describe, and modern science finds the term 'particles' totally inadequate. The word particle implies that the object in question is actually made of *something*, that it is some sort of solid. Yet what seems to us to be solid actually is not. Again, it is all a deception of our senses; we simply cannot grasp the truth with our limited faculties.

An atom, in very simple terms, is supposed to be made up of a

central nucleus of positively-charged electric particles called pro-
tons and of neutral particles called neutrons, with negatively-
charged particles called electrons circling in orbit around them.
If a thing exists at all, it is made of these atoms, and we therefore
say that it is made of some sort of material, that it is *matter*. However, the main part of an atom is not matter at all; it is empty space.
A more accurate description of 'matter' might be a series of holes
surrounded by electrical forces.

Hydrogen, the very simplest atom, has only one proton and
one electron. A basic substance which is not made of anything
other than itself is called an 'element'. Hydrogen is the simplest
of the elements. One hundred and three different sorts of elements have now been identified, ninety-two occurring naturally on
earth and eleven being man-made. If something is made of more
than one of these elements stuck together, it is called a 'compound'.

Matter is strange stuff; it is supposed to occupy space and have
weight. Conversely, anything that has no weight and cannot be
located in space does not exist physically; it is not a material thing.
Matter can take three forms, solid, gas or liquid, and it can be
made to change from one state to another. For example, a metal
can be changed into a liquid by heating it.

The human body—that mechanism which claims to be able to
feel touch—is a most complicated compound. A simplified
schoolchild's list of its contents reads as follows: oxygen, 65%; carbon, 18.5%; hydrogen, 9.5%; nitrogen, 3.3 %; calcium, 1.5%;
phosphorus, 1%; potassium, 0.35%; sulphur, 0.25%; chlorine,
0.2%; sodium, 0.15%; magnesium, 0.05%; and iron, iodine, zinc,
fluorine and other elements in traces. Put it all together, and we
still do not have that which thinks, that which 'lives'. It would
also be rather difficult, from this shopping list of ingredients, to
explain exactly what it is in that incredibly complicated compound
that is able to touch (we will consider this phenomenon in more
detail in a later chapter).

However, science does not stop at just discovering what the living and non-living things in this world are made of, or even what
their minutest atom is composed of; what it wants to know next is
what the constituent parts of the atom are made of. This leads to
the question of whether or not it is possible for there to be a smallest unit in the universe, or whether the division into ever-smaller

things goes on forever, a subject which we will further touch on in chapter seven.

Could we say that an electrical charge is matter? It doesn't seem to be. Many scientists these days go further and suggest that even the nucleus of an atom doesn't really exist as a material entity; it is simply the result of its positive and negative charges attracting each other. So we must be very careful not to assume that an atom of anything, be it as solid as iron, is really solid at all.

We touch many things, and are touched by many things, without being in the least aware of them. We do not normally feel the inner workings of our own bodies, for example. On the other hand, we feel a 'bump' when we come in contact with the large conglomerations of atoms that are recognizable to our naked eyes. Our backsides, which are largely made up of space, are able to perch successfully on the seat of a chair, which is also largely made up of space.

In other words, we are aware of existence on a particular 'plane' that seems to be strewn with other objects besides ourselves, which we can recognize and form an impression of with our senses, including our sense of touch. What we don't know, however, is whether or not there could be other 'planes of existence' running parallel to ours, maybe even occupying the same 'space' on a different level. The 'backside' of a hypothetical ghost or spirit entity, not being of the same atomic 'plane' as our own bodies, might go right through the chair, or even through us.

Can we say that the 'nothingness,' the 'space' of which atoms largely consist, exists? If you take a vacuum jar and pump out of it every single atom of air so that there is absolutely nothing left in it, would the 'inside' of that vacuum jar exist or not? If you think it would, what do you suppose it is? This question is really a mind-bender!

Unless we could suddenly be given equipment to register these atoms, as a radio set registers the radio waves that we can't normally hear, and which are passing through our rooms and our bodies all the time, we would never even know that they existed.

There could be myriads of things on planes different from our own which might be passing straight through us at this very moment. Maybe the single cells in our bodies, whose independent life cycles we normally do not think about at all, *do* somehow have a feeling that they belong to a great unit or 'whole,' even though they don't know what it is. What I mean is, does the cell on the end of your finger know that *you* exist?

Pantheistic philosophers maintain that we are all part of God in the same way, but that we are not normally aware of it. Islam rejects this notion, maintaining the distinct difference between the Creator and that which is created. Being able to touch, or being touched, is part and parcel of the created world of matter, and it is quite impossible for any of His Creation to touch God, for He is not a part of the world of matter; the attempts to imagine God as a physical Being are misdirected and cannot comprehend His actual Reality.

CHAPTER SIX

TIME

Whenever we contemplate God, we are confronted with the difficulty of apprehending His limitless nature. We live in a physical world bound by laws of nature which could have been created only by a Being *not* bound by those laws. To conceive of a Being who existed before and exists beyond the 'realities' of our physical world, a Being who is unaffected by the boundaries of matter, space and time, is beyond the scope of our experience and our imagination.

The passage of time is an aspect of our reality that has caused countless people to consider the existence of God. For, once we did not exist. Where were we before that time, and how did our existence come about? And, we all experience aging and realize that we will one day cease to exist. As all this is shrouded in the mystery of time, many attribute powers of life and death to time.

In the ancient world, time was personified as an eternal truth or divine entity, existing as one 'unit' in totality from eternity to eternity, encompassing everything within it, and having the ultimate power to triumph over everything because it alone reached 'forever'.

The Greeks gave the concept of time honorific treatment, personifying the inexorable passage of centuries as the figure of 'Old Father Time,' referring to 'him' as Kronos, the 'father' of Zeus and ultimately of all living things. And among the pagan Arabs, time (*Dahr*) was regarded as a god who existed from eternity to eternity and dispensed good or evil fortune to humanity.[6]

---

[6]The mistaken deification of time as opposed to the worship of the living God gave rise to the Arabic term '*dahriya*,' meaning an atheist or materialist.

This eternal existence of time is a notion that has been picked up in our modern atheistic and materialistic age. Rather than accept that there is a Creator-God, and a 'time' outside Time when the existence of created things had not yet begun, many scientists prefer the point of view that the particles from which the universe was formed had eternal existence; in other words, they did not have any beginning as such but went back to infinity.

Time is an integral part of our space, since it is something that is measured only by the interaction of one particle upon another, no particles, no time. Scientists who regard the universe as having no set beginning or moment of creation feel that the particles, albeit at a sub-atomic level, existed eternally as a kind of primeval soup, which, given infinite chronology (Kronos = time) somehow or other, by chance, formed themselves into whatever was necessary to get our universe going.

A similar notion might be that if one repeatedly threw a pile of bricks into the air for an infinite period of time, he or she might eventually end up with a desirable residence. Somehow it's hard to see how such an idea can be considered as less 'superstitious' or 'miraculous' than accepting the great designing Mind of a Creator!

Time becomes a problem to religious people when they start thinking about what it means to say that God is eternal and has existed forever. They claim that there never was any time when God did not exist, and that just as He goes back to infinity before our existence, so He goes on to infinity after our allotted span.

How can we gain any understanding of what infinite or eternal existence means? It just doesn't seem logical to us to think in terms that do not include a time sequence; as far as we are concerned, one thing always comes before or follows after another. An awareness of time is built into our nature; consequently, we find it very hard to understand what it means to say that God is outside time.

The passing of time is vital to our awareness of things. If you can grasp the idea that sound is simply a series of waves, then it is obvious that if you 'freeze' time at any one second and isolate a single one of these vibrations from all the rest, the sound at that point will not exist. To exist at all, it must spread out into space as a flow, and that involves time. We live in what is called a four-dimensional space-time continuum.

The passing of time adds a completely new dimension to our awareness of existence; without it, we could have no thought, no memory. We all feel that we know what time is since we can check off the passing minutes against the clock, but despite our comfortable notions and practical uses of it, precise time is something which, again, is really an illusion. It does not exist, except in the sense of a rather rough measurement which we use for our convenience.

We take our time from the length of the earth's journey around the sun, measured in units of the earth's revolving around itself. A complete orbit of the sun takes 365.24 units which we call days. Each day has twenty-four hours, each hour sixty minutes, each minute sixty seconds. But suppose we were counting by the moon, like the ancient Babylonians and Hebrews and Arabian tribes; then, if we were being exact, each month would have 29.5 days and each year only 354 days. Our attempts to get accurate measurements have brought us to the Cesium clock, but even that is a second off every few years. It really has proved incredibly difficult to accurately balance up our sun and moon.

Both the sun and the moon seem so paltry and small to astronomers when considering the distance involved in the measurement of the universe, that they talk of time 'by the stars' (Sidereal Time), or of 'light years'. One light year is the distance a ray of light can travel in 365.25 days at the incredible rate of 11,178,000 miles per minute, and the concept of that sort of speed or distance is beyond the understanding of most of us.

Looked at from another angle, it is important to bear in mind that our awareness of time is also subjective and depends on what we are doing. Who can say what five minutes really means? There is all the difference in the world between five minutes when one is waiting to be hanged, five minutes left of the football match when you need another goal, five minutes left in an exam when you still have an essay to write, five minutes too close to a fire, or five minutes sitting and relaxing on a park bench. What is the *real* five minutes worth?

Stop time at a particular moment — say 10:30 a.m. You may think you know what 10:30 a.m. means, but 10:30 a.m. is quite a different hour in Makkah or Sydney or New York, for while the sun is shining on one side of the earth, the other side is having its night. It all depends on where you happen to be.

And the timing of any event also depends on where you are looking from; it is relative to your position. If a Martian, a Venusian and a Plutonian all saw the earth blow up, the first two would see it a great deal sooner than the third. Their dating of the event would not record an 'absolute' date, but only the relative date in which it was registered in their particular time.

And what about the peculiar idea that if only one went fast enough, one would end up going backwards? How can it be? If you could put yourself into a circular orbit and travel at a speed faster than that of light, you would soon be able to see the back of your own head and would appear to shortly overtake yourself!

So, time is hard enough to contemplate, and when we try to work out what 'infinity' means, we really get into difficulties. Everything in our field of knowledge has beginnings and endings. But God does not.

We should try to understand that if God exists and is outside and beyond the whole of the created universe, then He must be able to observe the entire process simultaneously. It's a bit like the projectionist entertaining an audience frame by frame with a filmstrip, but having the ability to pull out the whole thing between his hands and see all of it at once. We measure our existence by the 'frames,' but God can see all of it simultaneously.

This would obviously mean that for God there would be no such thing as past, present or future as we know it. It would indicate also the truth of how, when we go to a totally different plane of existence outside our physical bodies, time is different. There is an increasing amount of evidence from people who tend the sick and dying that frequently, before their moment of final and total 'death,' their souls undergo a vast range of experiences, including sometimes a review of all the events and traumas of their earthly lives, that only takes a split second in terms of our time. The same elasticity of time is experienced by patients under anaesthesia or by people having dreams.[7]

On the other hand, when our loved ones 'die' and those left behind are yearning to be reunited with them, what seems to be a

---

[7]A well known film, 'Incident at Owl Creek,' was based on a sequence of adventures, occupying half an hour of actual viewing time, that took place in a condemned man's mind in the split second from the instant when he walked the plank to when he was hanged from a bridge.

very long time to the loved one left behind on earth may well pass in a flash for the so-called 'dead' person.

The biblical account of Creation has run into difficulties for those who wish to be scientifically respectable because it records God's starting from scratch or primeval chaos, with nothing but 'darkness upon the face of the deep,' and producing all the heavenly bodies, plus an up-and-running earth with all its life forms, culminating in man, in six days. No wonder He is said to have needed a rest on the seventh day!

While debunking the notion that the God 'who neither slumbers nor sleeps' ever needs to rest, the Qur'an also mentions that the creation took place in six days. However, it gives the clue that God's 'day' and ours is totally different. For example:

> God is the One Who created the heavens and the earth and everything between them in six days.....He governs (all) affairs from the heavens to the earth; then (in the end) it ascends to Him, on a day, whose measure is a thousand years of your reckoning. Such is He, the Knower of the Unseen and the Seen, the Mighty, the Merciful. (surah 32:4-6).

It is clear then that the 'days' of creation mentioned in both the Bible and the Qur'an obviously do not mean days as we reckon them, that is to say, the sun's twenty-four hour course around the earth. As one proof of this, if any is required, simply consider the fact that it refers to conditions which began before the earth and the sun were created. Chapter one of Genesis, for example, mentions God's creating a source of light (or energy?) on the first day and differentiating between light and darkness, but the creation of our sun and moon does not take place until day four!

As we have just seen, the Qur'an suggests in surah 32:5 that one of these 'days' is equivalent to a thousand years of our time (see also surah 22:47), and in surah 70:4, a 'day' is mentioned as being equivalent to no less than 50,000 years. On the whole, the Qur'an's revelations concerning time usually do not so much concentrate on notions of eternity as on the relativity of time.

> The angels and the Spirit [the Angel Gabriel] ascend unto Him on a day whose measure is fifty thousand years...

> They see it (the Day of Judgement) as far-off, but We
> [God] see it as near (surah 70:4, 6-7).

Here we are presented with three relative sorts of time: first,
human time, as measured by our sun and moon; second, the time
of living beings which are not specifically of this earth; and third,
that of God Himself. If we tried to measure God's time on the
plane of this life, it would take thousands of millions or even quin-
tillions of years. In the spiritual plane, however, all this 'time'
might pass in just a moment, in what the Qur'an refers to as 'the
twinkling of an eye'. What is of great importance here is that the
Qur'anic notion of time being relative is completely in keeping
with the latest scientific discoveries of the century and totally
unlike the notions presented in anthropomorphic mythology.

The pagan Arabs who worshiped time adapted the stoical attitude of those who do their best to cope with life despite their
depressing belief that death will be the end of everything. A typical pagan Arab statement was, 'What is there but our life in this
world? We shall die, and we live, and nothing but Time can
destroy us' (surah 45:24). The Qur'an utterly dismisses this attitude, pointing out that since humans have no idea of what will follow earthly death, they are merely making an assumption. 'And
they have no knowledge of that; it is mere supposition' (surah
45:24).

These pagans were arguing against the eternal teaching that
death is *not* by any means the end of an individual's story. All of
the religions founded on divine revelation, Judaism, Christianity
and Islam, have insisted that human beings have immortal souls
and bear responsibility for their actions in this life.

Such believers were generally mocked for what their non-
believing contemporaries insisted was wishful thinking. The skeptics maintained that as there was no proof for the life hereafter, it
could not possibly exist. The early Muslims, for example, were
challenged to bring back one of their forefathers from the dead as
proof that life continues after death (surah 45:25-26). Jesus, who
had earlier faced similar mockery, is reported to have commented
wryly that 'if they do not hear Moses and the prophets, neither will
they be convinced if someone should rise from the dead' (Luke
16:31).

In response to such skepticism, the Qur'an gives clear evidence for the survival of the soul after death, of creation and re-creation by God the second time, and of His ultimate power over all things. Time, based on the alternation of night and day, was only a part of His scheme. It was relative, but, nevertheless, in it there was a sign of God's creation and wisdom.

> Truly, in the heavens and the earth are signs for those who believe...and in the alternation of the night and the day, and in what God sends down from the sky as sustenance, and therewith revives the earth after its death....signs for people of intelligence (surah 45:3,5).

In short, the Qur'an demonstrates that the attitude of the pagans toward time was quite wrong, based as it was on their ignorance. Time, like everything else pertaining to our universe, is a created thing and not God. It does indeed have its share of mysteries, but it is no more eternal than matter. It is also relative to our conceptions and not absolute, as Einstein proved, and, in fact, is little more than a figment of our imaginations, a mere tool for measuring events in relation to each other. By definition, it can only be God who is self-subsisting, eternal from the beginning and eternal up to the end, the Absolute.

Time is one of the creations of God which everyone knows something about but none can fully explain. It can symbolize the destruction of everything physical, for everything 'breaks down' in time. It also symbolizes the great virtues of faith and patience, the two religious assets of believing humanity which alone are able to make sense out of time and also to overcome it.[8]

---

[8]As the Qur'an puts it: 'By Time, truly humanity is in loss, except for those who believe and do righteous deeds, and encourage each other in truth, and patience' (surah 103:1-3).

······························

CHAPTER SEVEN

GOD, THE NECESSARY BEING

Whatever is in motion is moved. If it is moved, it must have been set in motion by something which is already moving. That moving thing must have been moved by something else which was already moving, and so on to infinity. The whole of the universe is in motion, but this motion must have started somewhere. Whatever Immovable Mover it was that started it all in motion, this we call God. [9]

So runs the famous Christian argument attempting to prove the existence of God from the standpoint of science and philosophy. There are, in fact, many traditional ways of attempting to prove the existence of God based on cosmology — that is, on the study of the universe and its origin, function and causation. Some look for evidence of a Design or a Guiding Hand in the mechanics of space or in the progress of evolution.

An early line of thought, favored by St. Anselm in the eleventh century C.E.[10] and the great Muslim philosopher Muhyiddin ibn Al-Arabi in the twelfth, was the attempt to prove the existence of

---

[9]*Basic Writings of St. Thomas Aquinas,* ed. Anton C.Pegis, New York, Random House, 1945. For a discussion of Aquinas' five ways of proving the existence of God, see the following: *The Philosophy of Religion,* H.D. Lewis, E. Universities Press, 1965, pp. 157-165; *He Who Is,* E.L. Hascall, Longmans, chs. 4-6; *The History of Philosophy,* F.C. Copleshon, vol 2, ch 34.

[10]*The Ontological Argument,* A. Plantinza (Ed.) Anchor Books, *The Philosophy of Religion,* H.D. Lewis, p. 166.

God by logical reasoning alone. God was defined as the very essence of Perfection, Power, Goodness and Love. Therefore God, by definition alone, was by necessity the greatest possible thing that existed, the ultimate in the scale of values. Nothing greater than God could possibly be conceived of, for the simple reason that if anything could be thought of as more perfect or more good, then what had been simplistically thought to be God could not possibly be Him. If anything *were* greater, then God was not God. By definition, God had to be 'that other than which nothing greater nor more good can be conceived'.

In every walk of life there is a scale of values. Not everything is the same; some things are better or of more value than others, and some are worse. There is an ascending scale of good, better, and best. If God is the Absolute, the Best, then by logic He must exist; if He did not, then obviously many existing things could be thought of as being better or greater. It is absurd to think that that which is the greatest of all is imaginary. Therefore God is the Necessary Being and His non-existence is a logical impossibility.[11]

Likewise, if God is supremely perfect, He must exist because if He did not, He could hardly be described as being perfect. If He is not supremely perfect, then He cannot be God. Perfection must have existence as one of its qualities, since that which does not exist cannot be perfect. Therefore, God must exist. The whole argument is contained within the logic of its own statements.

At any rate it is evident from mankind's continued contemplation of God that He certainly *has* been persistently present in human consciousness, leaving some very tangible proofs of His existence as may be witnessed in the long history of prophethood through the ages. From where could the idea of God have originated if there had never been any such thing? How could the notion possibly have entered human consciousness at all without God's being the cause of it?

Science should be the ally of religion in considering this argument, for scientists will readily admit that the universe is full of phenomena and experiences which are, at present, still outside human consciousness and still awaiting our discovery. A humble scientist is deeply aware of how paltry and insignificant his knowledge really is, no matter how seemingly vast it may seem to be to

---

[11] *The Philosophical Review*, 1960, N. Malcolm.

the non-initiated.

The problem of attempting to prove the existence of God hinges upon what we mean by the word 'real'. For most people, anything 'real' is that which is subject to the laws of nature and limited by such elements as shape, mass, weight, position, and so on. If a thing is subject to any law of nature, then that law must be greater than it, and by the definition given above, it cannot be God.

This argument cannot, however, be used to prove that God does not have real existence, for we must admit that something far greater than any natural existing material object does exist — namely, the laws of nature. Surely the self-same argument that one would use to establish the existence and superiority of the concept of natural law to any physical thing is an argument basically similar to the argument for the existence of God, except that the argument for God's existence goes back a step further, for we cannot accept that the Power which created the laws of nature could be in any way limited by them.

In this case, the argument that God cannot have physical existence as we understand it is strengthened, since that would bind Him by His own laws. God is Real in the sense that He does exist and has limitless powers, although He does not exist as a limited physical object.

Our knowledge of any material thing is very limited, as we have seen, based as it is on the experience of our senses, which can make all sorts of errors. Now that we understand that matter is really only a manifestation of various forces of energy, isn't it possible that its physical existence in its many forms belongs to a realm of cause and effect which is not in itself physical at all, but which can somehow bring about physical reactions? Was St. Thomas Aquinas, after all, correct? Did an intangible God create a tangible world?

Materialists believe that only that which they can see with their eyes, hear with their ears, and feel with their hands is real. Religious thinkers, who take the opposite point of view, are given the 'umbrella' title of idealists. They look for the patterns of Mind behind the temporary and unstable appearances of matter, maintaining that that which is real cannot be seen at all. We can only glimpse a manifestation or impression of it, or measure its effects on its surroundings, but the thing-in-itself we can never see.

For example, if we consider a simple table, we may *know* that it is oblong in shape, brown in color and flat on the top, but we cannot in fact *see* that it is so. No matter from which angle we view it, we actually see it as anything but oblong, unless we deliberately poise ourselves in one single position directly centered above it. As for its color, we see it affected by light and shadow, so that bits of it may appear silvery and others black. We may *know* it is flat, but can only see the plane presented before our eyes and not the full shape in its many dimensions. In other words, we can see our impression of a table, but not the table-in-itself, the Real Table. Indeed, the whole thing may be an illusion or a hallucination; perhaps the table may not be there at all.[12]

Some philosophers maintain that the only thing we can know for certain is that we ourselves exist, and that, as we exist in an environment, there is something else outside of us which is *not* ourselves. However, some skeptics would maintain that, as we are unable to prove such a thing, perhaps we are merely entertaining some thoughts about things outside ourselves.[13]

Now, taking another train of thought, there is an argument for the existence of God based not on the notion of matter once it already exists, whatever that means, but on *causality*.

We observe in our universe that if anything at all happens, it happens for a reason; that is, it has been caused to happen by something else. These other 'somethings' existed before the event or thing they caused to happen. And they themselves were set in action by previous causes.

Contemporary scientists are grappling with the recent discovery that at the sub-atomic level there does seem to be a certain element of uncaused activity, which looks, at first sight, as if it might threaten the tidy notion that *everything* must obey set laws, because

---

[12]*Problems of Philosophy*, B. Russell, Oxford University Press, 1973, pp. 2-3; and *History of Philosophy*, NY, Simon and Schuster, 1945. Russell considered three fundamental questions: Is there physical reality at all? Does matter have real existence, and if so, what is its nature? What is the relationship between the Real Object, or the object-in-itself, and our experience of it? Our sense-data merely give us an 'appearance' of the reality based upon our own interpretation of the relationship between the Real object the object-in-itself, and our experience of it.

[13]Solipsists maintain that *nothing* has real existence except one's own mind.

everything is caused. However, against this unsettling notion it could be maintained that the apparent indeterminacy of sub-atomic reactions is no more than our ignorance. Once we have worked out the rules, it will be seen that all these apparently uncaused reactions *do* follow laws, after all.

It is worth saying over and over again that science never creates or invents anything; it simply discovers, when the mind-time is right for recognizing *whatever is already there*. The more 'clever' one imagines the discovering scientist to be, the more one should admit the Supreme Cleverness of whatever Power it was that set up the whole thing in advance, for brains to latch onto in due course!

If we put the theory of causation another way, we are saying that everything is as it is for a reason. In other words, everything is 'contingent'. A contingent thing is something that exists when it might not have. Take our table once again. We see the table and we assume that it exists. But is it possible that this table might never have existed? Of course it is. Consequently, it is a contingent thing. Why, then, does this table exist? Because someone chopped down a tree, took the wood and constructed it; if they had not done so, the table would simply never have been.

And what about the tree? Is that contingent? Might it be possible that that particular tree would never have existed? Again, of course it is. The tree exists simply because someone planted it, or some bird dropped its seed in its place, or some seed simply drifted there on the wind. There is a direct cause for this tree. And could that cause never have happened? Of course! And so it goes on. Every single thing in our universe is contingent.

What about the universe itself? Is it possible that the whole universe might never have existed? Yes, of course it is! It doesn't matter which scientific theory you start your case from—primeval soups, atoms colliding, Big Bang theories; they can all be put forward as possible causes for the universe's coming into existence, if you don't want to accept the simple possibility that God created it.

The trouble with many scientists is that they stop the argument there; they do not go on to the further step and ask whether the ingredients of the Big Bang, whatever that was, or whether any other causal theories, are themselves contingent. The answer has to be, 'Of course they are'. So, once again, we are landed on the shores of 'infinity'.

If you don't want to believe in God, you have to accept that everything goes on back and back to 'infinity'. There are really only these two choices: either we accept that the series of causes *does* go on and on forever, and that there is simply no such thing as the beginning of the universe and existence (or, presumably, an end to it, since infinity must surely stretch in both directions); or we submit and say that there *must* have been a very First Cause, and that there *was* some time when the universe had not yet been caused and therefore did not exist.

If you take this second view, you naturally wish to know what the First Cause might have been. This is what a believer would call the Moment of Creation—the moment when God said 'Be!' and it was so.[14]

Whatever you choose to call the Creative Force, that the universe does exist when it might not have is a simple fact, and that fact must, in all honesty, pose the questions 'Why?' and 'Whence?'

Just as a final mind-bender, I would like to share a couple of mathematical oddities which might illustrate the difficulties of accepting the word or concept 'infinity' at its face value. Greater brains than mine may be able to sort this all out, but I found it fun to juggle with these things.

Here's the first one, for which you really need a group of people with calculators of different makes. First of all, have a go at it with your own brain, and a pencil and paper.

All elementary mathematicians know what a third of something is; it is a perfectly easy fraction to contemplate. However, if you attempt to divide one by three, by a normal process of division, you will discover that you can *never* arrive at the answer. To smugly say '.333333333 recurring' is an excuse for an exact answer and does not really tell you the truth. Similarly, you can repeat the same process with the symbol pi, which is the equivalent of 22/7. Try doing the process by long division for a while and you'll see what I mean.

Now comes the fun, when we discover the lengths scientists go to in order to disguise problems and keep us happy. You wish to share your apple among three people. All right, you divide it by three. Do this by calculator, and you will see that you end up with .333333333 recurring. So, you become frustrated and decide to

---

[14] 'He said: 'Even so: God creates what He wills: When he has decreed a plan, He but saith to it, "Be," and it is !' (Qur'an 3:47).

eat the apple all by yourself after all. To get it back, simply multiply by 3 and all should be restored. But is it? The calculators which tell you the truth will give you .999999999 recurring, and you will be irritated to know that a piece of your apple has gone forever into 'infinity'. Other calculators, aware of this, make an automatic adjustment and give you back the whole number 3. But...

Is it possible for there to be a smallest particle? If it is, as a believer in creation would surely accept as an ultimate truth, then it should be possible to discover the size of a smallest number that cannot be divided any further. In other words, is it possible to have a number which cannot be divided by two? Now, by logic, the answer is 'No'. Even if you get down to a millionth trillionth of an inch, it can still in theory be divided by two. The only problem is that we run out of names to call this minuscule number. However, if you apply this to actual known distance, there seems to be a problem.

Before you can cross a distance of ten feet to reach a table, that distance can be halved and you must cross that half first. So you cross the first five feet. But before you travel this distance, that distance can be halved, so you cross the 2.5 feet first. Now, it is patently obvious that if it is true that numbers can be divided by two up to infinity, you are never, ever going to reach that table but will presumably get caught up in an infinite regression. However, being pragmatic, we know that we *do* reach the table. That must mean that somewhere we have crossed the smallest divide, and that, in theory, the theory of infinity is wrong, and there must be such a thing as a smallest particle.

If there is a smallest particle, where did it come from? Is it contingent? Need it never have existed? And so, on we go. What does all this prove? I don't know. I only know that there are more things in heaven and earth than we poor mortals have ever thought of, and that when we really try to grapple with these mind-benders, we may actually begin to *feel* the 'walls' that enclose our minds.

CHAPTER EIGHT

THE UNIVERSE, GOD'S SILENT BOOK

It's time we took a break from thinking about what we are and had a look at *where* we are. We seem fairly certain that we really do exist and that we are not just figments of imagination, because we are all aware that there is a 'we' which 'has' this imagination and that we can think. But we don't know for certain whether everything else around us is there or not, because our senses only give us subjective proofs, and all these other things really could be figments of our imagination. We could all be asleep or hallucinating, simply dreaming up the events and environments of our daily lives. However, being down-to-earth and sensible, we feel that our bodies are real, and that they do occupy space and have weight. So, where, exactly, are we?

Well, we know that we live on a large chunk of rock in space, which we call the planet Earth. We know that we are located fairly near a large shining silvery object that we call the Moon, and a big golden one called the Sun. We know that we have a special relationship with these two, for one goes in an orbit around us, and we both go in an orbit around the other.

Further away we see millions of tiny points of light which we call stars, and these all seem to be fixed in a set relationship with each other; for example, there is a famous group of three stars in a line which we call 'Orion's Belt,' and another group that looks something like the outline of a plough. They seem to have been like this since the beginning of time.

A very long time ago, some extremely observant people noticed that a handful of stars didn't seem to be fixed in a set relationship with their companions after all. When observed in relation to, say, Orion's Belt, they could be seen to approach it, and then to pass it by and leave it. The ancients noticed seven of these heavenly bodies that seemed to wander about on their own, and they were identified as the planets (from the Latin *planere*, to wander) Mercury, Venus, Mars, Saturn, Jupiter and Uranus. Mercury and Venus are nearer the Sun than we are, and the others are much farther away. Recent astronomy has since added two more to the list, Neptune and Pluto, deducing their existence from calculations and not from observation by the naked eye.

Now modern astronomy has ascertained that the zillions of stars in space are not really in fixed positions in relationship to each other, either; that is apparently nothing but an illusion. We cannot observe their movement with our own eyes because the distances involved are so vast that it puts observation off our time scale, but the truth is that although they may look quite 'still' and fixed in relationship to each other, they are actually hurtling away from us and from each other at inconceivable speeds.

The latest equipment can denote 'red shift,' parallax, vibrations and radio waves that indicate all sorts of exciting happenings going on in the night sky that looks so peaceful to our limited eyes. For space enthusiasts, there is a whole range of existence that is meaningless to the ordinary person, which includes neutron stars, black holes, quasars, pulsars and quarks.

When we begin to find out about these phenomena, we can only be amazed at the technical brilliance of our scientists who are making and computing all these discoveries. But we should pause to note that none of these things has been invented by these clever humans; they are simply discovering, when their brains and technology have become sufficiently mature enough to be able to cope with it, *what is already there.*

How did this amazing universe come into being? Does it simply exist and has it always been, or was there a time when it did not exist and when it was caused to be? Well, we have numerous theories concerning the matter, all based on the intuitions of the world's greatest scientists. Then there are the answers given by those who believe in God.

The sacred scriptures of Jews, Christians and Muslims all reject blind materialism that fails to see and feel the Hand of the Creator. Instead, they point to the eternal presence of God, Who is in full control of His creation, maintaining that there is nothing in the universe that is beyond His power, because He is its Planner, its Originator. They hold that it is nonsensical to suppose that the universe just happened by chance, especially when every observable thing within our experience obeys rules of cause and effect, providing clear evidence that it was created. The Qur'an, for example, states simply:

> When the Creator of the heavens and the earth decrees a matter, He merely says to it "Be!" and it is (surah 2:117; also 36:82 and 40:68).

Believers point out that all existing things, including ourselves, are contingent—that is, they might not have existed and only do so because it is God's will. For everything in the universe follows the laws of its Creator, 'Who created and then shaped; Who decreed and then guided' (surah 87:2-3; also 55:5-7, 10-12).

Sometimes rather simple human beings are happy to accept the idea that the universe was created by God, but they have a very paltry and inferior concept of what this God is like; they make Him a cozy anthropomorphic figure, almost like a benign old uncle. This may impart a comforting feeling, but it does not correspond to God's reality.

The Qur'an in particular raises the level of human understanding so that people may observe and grasp the true attributes of God and then reflect on His majesty and omnipotence. It does not give many specific details about astronomy or cosmology, but rather directs people to search and discover. When people start this search, trying to grasp the immensity of space and the wonders of creation and the intricate rules that govern it, then they may begin to realize that the universe is like a silent book for the advanced-level student. For the more one becomes aware of the realm of the Unseen (which Islam terms al-Ghaib, referring to the spiritual realm and its realities), the more one realizes that the physical universe contains parables and signs of a Creator-God who is amazing beyond belief.

One wonderful discovery is that the balance and uniformity of the Divine Law can be observed everywhere, from the vast reaches of the outer space of the cosmos to the microscopic realm. This reflects the Unity and Reality of the Creator, and also indicates that there are higher worlds beyond the material bounds of this physical universe.

Another important point is that God has apparently intended the human mind not to remain in ignorance, but to be able to grasp some of these laws through the intellect, something which no animal on this planet can do. The Bible tells of God's giving Adam the right to guard over and subdue everything on the planet, while the Qur'an mentions the concept of *sakhira*, meaning that everything in the heavens and on the earth was made serviceable for humanity. In other words, the implication is that human beings, through their intellects and endeavors, have a special relationship with the Creator, for they are able to discover and make use of the abstract laws governing the universe.

Perhaps there is in this a small proof that the human mind, which is gradually coming to understand the elements and forces of the universe, and is steadily advancing higher and higher in spreading its influence and control over these physical laws, is, in fact, a sign of the Supreme Mind which controls, governs and directs all physical phenomena and systems in the universe. Scientists should always, however, avoid the temptation of believing they fully understand everything. As Galileo commented, 'I always accounted as extraordinarily foolish those who would make human comprehension the measure of what Nature has a power or knowledge to effect, whereas on the contrary there is not any least effect in Nature which can be fully understood by the most speculative minds in the world!'

These physical laws form a stable and regular system, even if it is complex beyond our present powers of understanding. Indeed, every scientist, whether he or she believes in God or not, has absolute faith that the laws of the universe indeed represent one overall system, every piece of which fits into the intricate design with perfect logic and necessity.

Now, if that is the case, the believer has a strong indicator that the universe, and especially life as we know it, did not just come about by chance. When one examines that juxtaposition of some of the universal laws, it presupposes a strong influence that one might call 'antichance'.[15] Take, for example, the existence at the same time of both the second law of thermodynamics and the

---

[15]See *Issues in Science and Religion*, I.G. Barbour, SCM Press, 1966, p. 387.

existence of life on our planet.

The second law of thermodynamics states that there is an interchange of heat from one thing to another until equilibrium is reached. In our universe, this takes place all the time, and this heat-level at equilibrium is far too low to sustain life forms as we know them. And yet, life does exist on this earth, even though the environment of space is so hostile that on the very next nearest chunk of rock, the Moon, no person could possibly live for a second without a survival space suit. The Sun, for example, could burn into ashes all that exists on this planet and turn it into cosmic dust; the slightest imbalance in the Earth's revolution would result in the destruction of all life. No scientist doubts for a moment that there are established laws which account for this seeming miracle, even though they might not wish to call the originator of those laws God.

Let's go off on a slightly different tack and contemplate for a moment not just the existence of the universe, but our own position in it. When we try to pinpoint our exact position in the universe, we find that we have a problem. Our sun is a star. The planets surrounding us constitute the solar system, and our solar system is part of a very large group of stars called a galaxy. There are believed to be millions of galaxies in space, and our galaxy, called the Milky Way, is estimated to have about a hundred million billion stars in it. On a clear night you can see our star neighbors all clustered together in the sky.

All these matters are fairly well-known today, but this was not always the case. Astronomers of the Middle Ages, basing their ideas on the system worked out by Claudius Ptolemy in the third century after Christ, conceived of a fairly small universe with the Earth in the exact center, and the Sun and Moon and our known planets traveling around it in circular orbits, a conviction that was very agreeable to human beings who wished to believe that they were the highest order of creation, the center of everything, and that everything existed for their benefit. Beyond this neat arrangement was 'the edge of the universe,' some kind of barrier or rim that was called the Fixed Sphere, in which all the stars were embedded, which accounted for the way they always traveled around the sky in set relationships to each other. Beyond that, there was nothing. Everything was perfect, regular, circular, and very carefully worked out by God.

Then suddenly, later scientists came to the realization that their calculations did not quite correlate with this simple picture, and they began to work out theories that were startling in their implications. For example, the astronomer-monk Copernicus (1473-1543) stated that the universe did not orbit around our Earth; instead, our Earth was orbiting around the Sun.[16]

This had far-reaching implications. Once human beings adjusted to the shock of the thought that they could no longer claim to be the center of everything, the unsettling consideration arose in the minds of the bold that possibly the planets and stars were not all created just for our benefit. We got knocked out of our glorified, all-important, central position and began to feel rather small and troubled by our insignificance as a result.

Next, it was discovered that the Earth was not a special planet, but just one unit in a system of planets, and that, compared to some of the others, it was very small. Indeed, scientists were short- ly forced to admit that it constituted an infinitesimally small part of the universe. There might be millions of other planets out there, all with life forms on them.

The Christian Church was particularly upset by this; it had always taught that man was the last word in God's creation, God's very image and likeness. But how could this be so when he was just an insignificant inhabitant of an unimportant and tiny planet that was one among millions? It was a shattering thought.

If these new discoveries of science and astronomy were really true, how could human beings possibly be of any importance to God? There were very likely other conscious beings living on these other planets, and these might be much more important to God than ourselves. Who could tell? In any case, even if it could be imagined that the human race as a whole had any importance what- soever to that distant Divine Force, the Almighty could hardly be expected to be in the least bit concerned with humans as individu- als! It would be even more outrageous a claim than supposing that there was a Master Gardener in charge of the whole earth who was intimately concerned with the fate of one tiny ant, or each individ- ual baby spider on one of those trails of myriad gossamer threads!

As if these discoveries were not enough to make believers very

---

[16]For a discussion on medieval scientific theory, see *The World of Copernicus*, Angus Armitage, Signet Science Library, p. 78.

uncomfortable, they were subsequently to be completely shattered by the findings of modern astronomy, for as soon as the telescope was invented, scientists began to make tremendous discoveries. One astronomer, Giordano Bruno (1548-1600), insisted that space was without end and that therefore it was ridiculous to think that our Sun could be in the center of it. If space was endless, there could be no center at all.

Bruno supposed that all the stars were suns, each with its own planets. The Christian Church took a very dim view of such subversive theories and had Bruno examined by the Inquisition. The astronomer stood up for what he believed and died by burning at the stake.[17]

Another leading scientist pounced upon by the Inquisition was the brilliant Galileo Galilee (1564-1642). His astronomical observations implied that there was no end to the things waiting to be discovered with the aid of the new telescopes, and that humanity would have to completely relinquish its old, comfortable notions about the universe. All at once, humans beings were forced to realize that they knew hardly anything about it at all!

One of Galileo's new discoveries so upset the Church that teachers were not allowed to mention it for over a century. This was the discovery that the Sun had 'spots,' now known to be solar flares. These spots were originally thought of as blemishes, and the idea of a 'spotty' sun apparently implied to the Church that it was not perfect. This in turn was seen as a criticism of God's ability to create all things in perfection and was therefore considered blasphemy.

As a result, Galileo was actually forced by the Inquisition to 'admit' that he had been propagating lies, and not until he was on his death-bed did he dare to repeat his outrageous statements and insist he had been telling the truth all along.

People used to be terrified of eclipses, comets or meteorites, regarding them as psychic portents of disaster or of some untoward happening sent by God, their flashes across the sky marking out the births of great and heroic humans. But in the sixth century after Christ, the prophet Muhammad (pbuh)[18] declared that

---

[17]See *The World of Copernicus*, Angus Armitage, Signet Science Library, p. 80.

[18]The letters 'pbuh' stand for 'peace be upon him' and are used by Muslims with the names of the prophets.

such things were not supernatural portents, but simply natural phenomena, appearing by God's will. There was an eclipse of the Sun on the day when the Prophet's infant son Ibrahim died, and people connected it with his death. The Prophet (pbuh) stood for a long time and led the people in prayer. When the Sun was bright again, he said: 'The sun and the moon are not eclipsed on account of anyone's death or birth, but they are two of Allah's signs. He produces awe by means of them. When you see an eclipse, hurry to prayer' (Abu Dawud). Centuries later, Edmond Halley (1656-1742) affirmed that meteorites were just chunks of rock in space that had their own orbits, and if they happened to crash down upon earth from time to time, it was because of the orbits of earth and meteorite coming together by the inexorable laws of the space-time continuum.

The progress of science could not be halted by the panic of the Church fathers, for science was not destined to become a tool of the Church in promoting its dogma. During this period, Muslim scientists carried the torch of knowledge. Their ranks included such names as al-Farghani (Alfraganus), al-Nayrizi (Anaritius), Abu Abdullah al-Battani (Albategrius), Ibn al-Haythem (Alhazem), al-Zarqali (Azarqiel), Nur al-Din al-Bitruji (Alpetragius), and many others. None of these doubted for one moment the Hand of the Creator, manifested in the universe.

It was soon reasoned out that the Fixed Sphere didn't exist at all, that the stars were very much farther away than had been previously believed, and that there were millions and millions of miles of unknown space. It was also realized that the idea of circular celestial orbits was nonsense and that everything was in a state of change. Possibly the stars were actually rushing away from us at incredible speeds.

In the year 964 C.E., Abd al-Rahman al-Sufi reported the presence on the celestial sphere of the faint light of another galaxy, in the constellation Andromeda. It was not until 1923, however, that Edwin Hubble stumbled across its real nature—a galaxy like our own, lost in the vastness of extragalactic space. To make this discovery, he used the largest telescope available at that time. Since then, surveys have suggested a hundred billion galaxies, stretching to billions of light years away. Compared to the volume of the universe as it was understood in the last century, the universe is now known to be a million billion times larger.

In terms of the scale of the universe that is now accessible to large telescopes, galaxies are mere grains of dust, uncountable in the tremendous depths of the cosmos. Yet galaxies, giants and dwarfs alike, contain between one and a hundred billion stars, separated from each other by light years. Thinking of the numbers and distances is mind-boggling; for example, our sun is 30,000 light years from the center of our galaxy and, travelling at 250 kilometers per second, it takes 250 million years to complete one orbit!

Gigantic explosions were observed — the supernova. Stars were dying. We, too, were hurtling along blindly toward an unknown doom. In the face of all this, some believers in religion came to question their most basic beliefs, while others gave up belief altogether. Was God's Creation going wrong? A shred of hope was offered when scientists suggested that, if some stars were dying, it might also be true that others were still being created, and the theory of Continuous Creation was born.

All these fears were based on an incorrect and limited knowledge of the universe and the wonderful workings of the Power behind it. The Christian Church in particular wished to preserve belief in what was stated in the Bible. If the scientists were correct, it would mean that not only was God's work *not* finished in six days, as is stated in the Book of Genesis, but that it is nowhere near being completed, even now. And if the Church was wrong about this, how many other things was it wrong about?

If you began to think about it, where exactly in the universe was God supposed to be? There was no longer any locus for Him. Since there was no fixed perimeter and space was endless, one could no longer imagine the created universe as a perfect sphere having everything contained within it, cradled in God's almighty Hands. And all of a sudden it became fashionable not to believe in God at all. Many men of science found the whole idea of religion to be complete nonsense, its arguments and dogmas irrelevant and simplistic, and they became atheists.

The questions of how the universe began, or how it was built or designed and what its future was, became the searching ground of atheists as well as believers, scientists confidently expecting that they would find a secular answer to these questions which did away with the 'superstitious hypothesis' that there was a Creator-God.

When these questions are asked of a cosmologist today, the

answer is usually couched in the language of the accepted model of our time, the so-called Big Bang theory; this is the logical extension of the discoveries about galaxies receding from Earth at phenomenal speeds. If they are shooting 'away,' then they must have been closer together yesterday. And if you follow the process backwards to its 'beginning,' there must have been a time when all the material of the universe was condensed into one gigantic atom, which then exploded.[19]

What this theory does *not* tell us, of course, is how this atom originated, how it got there, what space it occupied, and why it 'banged'. All these and many other questions about this or other theories concerning the origin of the universe, such as the Steady-State theory, remain completely unanswered. Obviously, the moment one accepts the notion that the universe actually did have a beginning in time, one must inevitably return to the vexing question of the creation and the nature of the Creator.

---

[19]For discussion on modern theories, see *The Nature of the Universe*, Fred Hoyle, Oxford, Basil Blackwell, 1960, and *Issues in Science and Religion*, I.G. Barbour, SCM, 1966, p. 367.

CHAPTER NINE

THE ARGUMENT FROM DESIGN

The theory of evolution is taught almost universally in the Western world as a fact and not as a theory. When it was first publicly formulated independently by two scientists, Charles Darwin (1809-1882) and Alfred Russel Wallace (1823-1913), the Christian Church was congratulating itself on its own new 'scientific knowledge'. Previously Archbishop Ussher of Armagh (1581-1657), with a talent for biblical calculations, had actually worked out the year of creation as 4004 B.C., and now Dr. Lightfoot of Cambridge had fixed the exact time, concluding that God had finished all the life forms by 9 a.m. on Friday, October 23rd.[20] Although this sounds ridiculous now, at the time, the scholarly archbishop was very pleased with his results, and the Church was mightily annoyed that along should come some troublemaker with intent to spoil this neat knowledge.

Unlike the atheistic and irreligious attitude prevalent in much of the West today, a century ago people took their faith very seriously; prior to that time, no one had seriously challenged the biblical narrative or tried to prove it wrong. Indeed, up until the end of the Middle Ages, most of the leading scientists in the Western tradition had been monks and churchmen.

Even the great scientist Sir Isaac Newton (1643-1727) had agreed entirely with biblical teachings; in fact, he wrote his great work on the principles of mathematics as a commentary on Psalm 19.[21] Regarding the evidence of extinct species that had once

---

[20] *Issues in Science and Religion,* I.G. Barbour, SCM, 1966, p. 97.

[21] Newton calculated the mathematical proof for the elliptical orbit of planets. It began as a 24 page calculation and expanded into a work

lived on the earth, he believed that they must have been killed off in the great flood at the time of Noah; they were the unlucky ones that did not get into the Ark.

During this period, individuals who were not inclined to believe in the story of the Flood had to deal with the findings of a group of enthusiasts called Neptunists, who used the 'evidence' provided by fossilized shells found on a mountain top to 'prove' the fact of the biblical disaster and that the waters of God's anger had once covered the whole world.

However, biologists and geographers were becoming more and more disenchanted with these ideas, and they accused the people who took the Bible stories literally of being simpletons and 'cranks,' tossing out a lot of sarcastic comments to make them look stupid. For example, many species of animals that are now extinct were found in America by early explorers. How did they get across the Atlantic Ocean? And what about the strange animals found in Australia which don't exist anywhere else—the kangaroo, the emu, and that weird warm-blooded, egg-laying mammal with a duck's bill and flippers, the duck-billed platypus? Had they come into existence all by themselves? And anyway, if you counted up all the living species and discounted the extinct ones, there were so many species still in existence that it was impossible to imagine how Noah could have fit them all inside the Ark.

Georges, Comte de Buffon (1707-1788), made a study of the erosion of land. He was particularly fascinated by the discoveries of the movement of the earth's crust. Newly-created rock seemed to be continually thrusting up from the molten core of the earth, pushing existing continents farther and farther apart. Actually, if you look at a flat atlas of the world, you can see how the major land masses might once have fitted together and formed one huge continent, like a giant jigsaw puzzle. Where two beds of very hard rock were pushed together, one either had to slide under the other, or, if they met head-on, both were pushed upwards and formed steep-sided mountains (if you push your fingertips together you'll see what he meant).

---

in three volumes: *The Mathematical Principles of Natural Philosophy*. The universe was a single coherent system of amazing clarity, operating in faultless precision according to Divine Law. His scientific theories were not superseded until the late nineteenth century, with the new Theories of Relativity.

So, perhaps the tops of mountains had once been the bottom of oceans and had been pushed up by the movements of the land. If this were so, the idea of the Great Flood as the cause of seashells' being found on mountaintops became unnecessary, for a perfectly natural explanation for this already existed.

Pious Christians were on the whole very reluctant to let go of their old traditional beliefs. The fact that so many did so demonstrates the sheer strength of the arguments being put forward against the mythology of the Bible. Materialist scientists had to fight against them each step of the way, and many people who had previously believed every word of the Bible to be literally true felt grossly disloyal and as miserable as traitors when they were reluctantly obliged to shed those beliefs.

The scientists were not particularly *trying* to destroy belief in God; if that occurred, it was merely a corollary of their findings and not the deliberate intent. However, they found themselves unable to accept any longer the pious principle that if a biblical narrative went totally against all known facts and logic, it was nevertheless their duty to believe it as an 'act of faith,' and if they patently did *not* believe it, they were sinners destined for damnation.

The invincible armor that the scientists possessed, which enabled them to 'conquer' biblical mythology, was the fact that they were inexorably following logic and reason, and that they were being true to themselves. Gradually, the blinding light of scientific fact was forcing long-cherished beliefs in ancient myths to retreat and be replaced by rationalist materialism.

The argument was then put forth by some that one could still accept the *principles* of what the myths were intended to teach, but not the details; in other words, while the narrative or story might not be literally true, what was important was not its historical detail but the lesson it conveyed. The trouble with this approach was that it undermined confidence in the entire text, as it became increasingly difficult to know which bits were 'true'.

Many people in the West were not convinced by such materialist arguments, which undermined the credibility of the Bible and hence seemed to undermine the idea of belief in a perfect God. They retained their strong faith in a personal God, the Source of Divine Love who sees the smallest sparrow fall and knows us so intimately that even the hairs on our heads are numbered. In defense of God as the Creator, the Rev. William Paley (1743-1805), for example, argued in his book, *Natural Theology*, that every single thing on earth was so perfectly fitted to its natural environment that it was impossible for this to have occurred by chance. One could not simply throw up a handful of bricks into the air and expect them to fall down into the perfect and finished shape of a house, not even if one threw the bricks a million million times. For a house is *designed*; it is much more than a random assembly of bricks.

Paley also used the analogy of a watch. What is a watch? he asked. Well, it is something that tells us the time. But really, if you take the watch apart, it is just a collection of bits and pieces, springs and coils, cogs and wheels. A child could play around with them for ages and amuse himself by creating patterns with it, or an artist could create a work of art with its pieces. But only when it is put together in one specific way does it take on another function altogether: it begins to tell the time!

This could not have come about by accident; it had to be designed. Moreover, the fact that there is such a thing as 'time,' which obeys laws and can can be measured, was a pre-existent condition for the creation of a machine for performing that task. The concept of 'watch' implies a knowledge and understanding of certain intangible but existent concepts, intelligible only to a higher mind. The need to tell the time was not the reason why those cogs and coils were created, but it *was* the reason the *watch* was created.

If you wandered through some pleasant valley and found a heap of stones, you would think nothing about them but that they had arrived at their present place through natural causes. But if one day you came across other stones that were arranged in such a way that they formed the words, 'Welcome to Kansas City,' you would not imagine that this had happened by chance or accident, but would assume that some designing mind had arranged them in this manner—a mind that understood the concept of communication of one mind to another through language, and such intangible things as the meaning of the concept of 'welcome'.

In nature, every creature fits so perfectly into its environment that surely it cannot be accidental. Consider the eye of a bird, for example. A bird needs to pick up seeds and small insects, yet also to soar in the sky and see great distances; therefore it needs both far and near vision. And it does have both. If either were only partially developed or still evolving, the bird would fail to survive. Again, the archer fish needs an eye that can cope with refraction from the surface of the water, as well as the ability to shoot out a jet of liquid at the correct angle to knock down its prey, and it has both. If any of its faculties were only partially developed, the archer fish would not be here.

Hence, one of the major arguments in favor of the existence of God is known as the Argument from Design. It is really based on the law of cause and effect. Most people would agree that, had things been different, the universe need never have existed at all. Every single thing that exists does so for a reason; it was caused by something. Therefore, the fact that the universe as a whole exists, when it might not have, suggests that there must be a reason for the existence of it in its entirety. What could this reason possibly be?

If we define the universe as everything that is, then the cause of its entire existence must lie *outside* the universe itself, a First Cause that is not in itself any part of that which it caused. The alternative to this idea would have to be that all the natural laws governing the creation and maintenance of the universe came into being by pure chance. Since the design is so intricate and so perfect, the chances of this chance seem so remote as to be classifiable as 'impossible'.

Scientists trying to create 'life' in test-tubes know perfectly well that they can be successful in their experiments only if a great number of very special conditions occur at just the right time, in just the right proportions, under just the right conditions. These do not occur at random, and scientists use extreme care, effort and skill to set up these very conditions, according to their discovered knowledge and technology.

It is quite useless to claim that if all the ingredients were just thrown together and left (assuming, of course, that a selection of ingredients to remove any unwanted ones had occurred first, which would certainly be cheating), in infinite time the desired result would come about by chance. There is no proof whatsoever for this rather remarkable assertion; it actually requires considerably more faith to believe in that than it would take to believe in God. If the required effect *did* appear to happen 'just spontaneously,' one would suspect the very strong possibility of what one might call 'antichance,' or 'loaded dice'!

Some scientists try to suggest that the origin of life was not on this earth anyway, but somewhere in outer space—but this only pushes the problem further back, and into a much more forbidding setting. Outer space is exceedingly hostile to life; therefore, it seems highly unlikely that life should arise spontaneously within it, and then land on earth, where the conditions for life have proved ideal.

In 1953, Stanely Miller caused excitement when his experiments passed an electric spark through a collection of hydrogen, methane, ammonia and water vapor, which he presumed simulated conditions at the beginning of life on earth. His efforts did manage to produce four amino acids; thus it was claimed that the building-blocks of life had been created in the test-tube!

However, forty years further on, no scientist has yet been able to produce the full twenty amino acids needed. Scientists also point out that there is an 'oxygen factor' to consider. If there had been oxygen in the primitive 'air,' the first amino acid could never have occurred; yet without oxygen, if it had occurred, it would have been destroyed by cosmic rays. The same energy that splits up compounds in the atmosphere would very quickly decompose any complex amino acids that formed 'by chance'. Miller himself had to admit that once he had created his four amino acids, he had to very quickly remove them from the area of the spark, which would have decomposed them.

Furthermore, there are now around a hundred known amino acids in existence, of which only the specific twenty are needed to form life; moreover, these twenty are all in what is known as the 'left-handed' shape. The extreme improbability of this occurring spontaneously might be compared to the likelihood of your randomly selecting, from a pile of millions of a hundred different kinds of buttons in two different 'sets,' or, let's say, colors, only the twenty varieties you require and no others, all in the one specific 'set' or color.

Statisticians have now calculated that since the proteins needed for life have very complex molecules, the 'chance' of one forming at random is in the region of ten to the power of 113—a number larger than the estimated total of all the atoms in the universe! On top of that, no less than two thousand proteins serving as enzymes are needed to speed up the chemical reactions in each cell, and without this help the cell would die.[22]

---

[22]*Issues in Science and Religion*, I.G. Barbour, SCM, 1966, p. 387, and *Human Destiny*, Le Comte De Nouy, Longman's Press, New York, 1947.

The structural units of DNA involve five histones (basic proteins) governing the activity of genetic material. The chances of forming even the simplest of these is said to be around twenty to the power of one hundred, another fantastic number. Moreover, proteins depend on DNA for their formation, but DNA cannot form without pre-existing protein. Which came first, the chicken or the egg? They must have developed *in parallel*, or evolved simultaneously, without either coming originally from the other.

As the biologist Edwin Conklin put it: 'The probability of life originating from accident is comparable to the probability of the unabridged dictionary resulting from an explosion in a printing shop' (*Reader's Digest*, January 1963, p. 92).

Another point: it is also unlikely that life arose in water by chance. Water is not at all conducive to the necessary chemistry, as it breaks up large molecules rather than encouraging them to build up. In other words, there is little scientific evidence that favors the building up by chance of any primeval organic 'soup'.

Thus, there seems to be undeniable evidence of purpose in it all. Many material things, which have no powers of thought or intelligence themselves, seem to cooperate somehow to produce ordered and stable systems, out of which all sorts of possibilities, such as life and consciousness, can arise. They seem to be achieving a purpose which they cannot possibly be consciously bringing about themselves.

There must surely, therefore, be a Designer or God whose intelligence actually guides things to achieve certain aims. It's all very well for scientists to suggest that in the 'primeval soup' of atomic particles in the universe, everything suddenly—or even over a vast period of time—sorted itself out to form the basis of our existence. But the conditions would all have had to existed prior to the fragments, and everything would have had to have

---

De Nouy was a mathematical genius who worked on the possibility of creating one molecule of protein containing only 2,000 atoms (instead of its normal much higher number) by chance. He further suggested accounting for only 2 different kinds of atoms in this molecule instead of 4, as in reality. He estimated that with 500 trillion 'shakes' per second, the time needed to form one such molecule by chance could be 10 to the power of 242 billion years. Since the earth has existed for around 2 billion years, and the possibility of life on it for only around 1 million, de Nouy concluded that chance creation was therefore impossible.

come together at exactly the right moment. The 'primeval soup' theory totally ignores any explanation of where the original atoms came from anyway. And it is worth remembering that the vast majority of the laws of the universe are actually hostile to life as we know it; so the fact that life exists at all requires some plausible explanation in terms of antichance.

CHAPTER TEN

THE THEORY OF EVOLUTION

The Darwinian theory of evolution has been one of the most powerful of the forces behind the growth of materialism. In the West, it is usually presented to children in schools as an essential fact, rather than as a theory or a working hypothesis.[23]

The geological evidence given in support of evolution seems very convincing to a young student, but this is largely because no evidence to support the other side of the argument is ever seriously presented. The theory of evolution basically presupposes that all nature has arrived at its present form because the more efficient designs always ousted the less satisfactory ones by depriving them either of life or of a food supply. The survival of the fittest was nature's great aim, although what nature was, and how this aim was really achieved, remained a matter of faith.

The theory is repugnant to believers in God for several reasons. Firstly, of course, it is repugnant because it rules out the existence of God altogether, postulating a universe which has no Divine Being as its Creator and Guide. Religion is treated as superstition, and it becomes the scientist's duty to try to educate religious people out of their ignorance toward 'mature thinking'.

Secondly, the theory is repugnant when applied to human beings, because it is a theory of progress that sets a premium on

---

[23]See *The Orion Book of Evolution,* Jean Rostand, 1961, p. 95, and *Evolution, Creation & Science,* Fraub Lewis March, 1947, p. 10, 'It is not that they are aware of the difficulties ... and esteem them of little weight or importance; they never heard of them and are amazed at the bare possibility of the accepted theory being criticized' (C.P. Martin in *American Scientist,* January 1953, p. 105).

sex and greed; on a subhuman level, it is a process that cares for nothing but success. The weak 'go to the wall' and are wiped out by the millions.

In human terms, survival of the fittest means that anyone who thinks he is a specimen of the fittest has the right to stomp on the faces of everyone else. One can immediately see why this theory was seized upon and promoted by the Nazis prior to World War II, when they were deliberately trying to manipulate genetics in order to create the master race, the *herrenvolk*.

By extension, this theory also implies that since the development of the world is presumably governed by chance and there is nothing else to account for it, individuals may use their short lives to the best of their advantage and trample upon anyone who stands in their path.

How did this theory first come into being? Well, the economist Thomas Malthus (1766-1834) studied the principles of population and wrote a famous essay pointing out that the size of any animal community was based on its food supply.[24] According to him, it was common that many more babies were born than could possibly survive on the food available; hence, a struggle to live would necessarily ensue in which the weakest were defeated by those who could use the advantage of size or savagery or speed or cleverness. Only the most fit would survive, and the rest would cease to exist.

When Charles Darwin read Malthus' work, he suddenly realized that the ability of life forms to adapt themselves to their environments was really the key to their existence or extinction. If a species developed to perfection to fit a particular climate and its vegetation, and that environment suddenly changed, the species would immediately find itself at an enormous disadvantage and might even die out. For example, it has been suggested that the cold-blooded dinosaurs, who ruled the world for millennia, were unable to adapt to the ice age, whereas the smaller, warm-blooded mammals could. So dinosaurs died out and rabbits survived. The force that selected which creatures should live and which should die was nothing other than nature itself.

Since those creatures with the most favorable characteristics survived at the expense of the others, it was suggested, it was only a matter of time before they formed the majority and the less fit

---

[24] *On the Principles of Human Population*

decreased in number and finally became extinct. One was therefore forced to accept either that God had rather pointlessly created myriads of species that were doomed to failure (which might
imply that God's plans were going wrong), or that it was possible
for species to change and develop, in which case God's original
plans were being improved upon and the species were not fixed
once and for all at the time of Creation. This was the implication
of the theory of the Mutability of Species, put forward by Darwin.

It was found, moreover, that it was quite possible to deliberately change the shape and size and marketability of domesticated
animals by artificial selection, thereby deliberately breeding creatures that could produce more meat with less fat, or more eggs
and more milk, at greater speed.

Darwin then considered man, to him just another animal. Did
human beings vary like other animals? Did they also increase so
rapidly that they competed for existence? Did their bodies show
traces of their animal descent—for example, such elements as
bones that were rudiments of tails? Could their special qualities of
mind and morals have appeared naturally as they slowly changed
form? To all these questions, Darwin and those who thought like
him answered an emphatic 'Yes'.

Darwin's main point was that the struggle for existence and
fight for survival would gradually lead to progress and higher
development; consequently, man could well afford to feel proud
of his ascent from very humble origins. The idea that man had
been created perfect, but had sadly fallen from his state of grace
into sin and imperfection, could no longer be sustained.

The idea of evolution implies the incorrectness of the belief
that God had made all the different species of animals perfect at
the moment of creation. According to this view, each living thing
did not spontaneously appear, perfectly created to fit the environment, but developed out of another living thing that came before
it. And it was not simply suggested that one living thing was
imperfect at any stage during its progress toward something else,
but it was also implied that even the environment was not perfect
and finished, for it too kept changing, and as it changed the creatures that were most fitted for the new conditions survived while
the others did not.

Once a species has come into existence, it seems to be able to
develop in limited ways toward certain goals. People who believe

this to be possible but also believe in a divine force are known as vitalists. They accept that there *is* change from one stage of development to another, but hold that this change is *caused* by something beyond our universe, which guides it; in their view, the development of any organism is always toward some sort of goal or end.

Ever since the publication of Darwin's famous books, *On the Origin of Species*, in 1858, and *The Descent of Man*, in 1867, scientists have generally refused to accept the theist notion that God made everything just as He wanted it to be forever. People who clung to the old teachings were laughed at, even though they tried to offer scientific explanations for their beliefs.

If Darwin were correct, then humanity would have to abandon its belief in the fixity of species and assume a vast lapse of time since the origin of life; abandon the idea of the infinite wisdom and munificent kindness of God in perfectly adapting every creature to the surroundings in which it must live; admit that humans descended from animals and give up the biblical teachings about original sin; and try to guess at what stage in all this the animal-human gained his soul—if such a thing existed at all. Presumably, human beings could no longer claim to have any sort of special relationship with God. Indeed, it might be true that there was no God after all.

The founders of communism, Marx and Engels, were absolutely delighted with Darwin's theories, and Engels identified the struggle for the dignity of humanity with a struggle against religion and its untruthful pretenses.[25] He looked forward to the creation of a race of supermen, as far removed from modern humans as they were from the ape, believing that religion would be unmasked as a fake and believers shown up as ignorant, decadent, and negative in their attitude towards human progress. So communism set about deliberately undermining religion for the greater good of humanity.

It is no wonder, therefore, that the Christian Church leaders, faced with all this, became convinced that Darwinism, socialism, communism, materialism and atheism were all virtually identical, and all equally the work of the devil!

---

[25]See *Charles Darwin*, Sir Gavin de Beer, Oxford University Press, 1958, p. 215.

But let's take a fresh look at some of the 'facts' that seemingly implied an irreparable schism between science and religion. For a start, we should remember that the geological record contains the remains of only such animals as happened to die in suitable places. It can never be even approximately complete, and evolutionary 'sequences,' although they may look very convincing in a textbook, have of necessity great gaps in them which have been filled by mere supposition.

The 'expert' may point to cases such as the changes that are believed to have occurred in the gradual loss of the extra toes in the hooves of ancient horses, for example, but it is still nothing more than an inference that this phenomenon was, in any real way, related to the survival of the fittest.

In fact, it is generally believed that we have the complete fossil series from eohippus to horse, and archaeopteryx to bird, but museum exhibits of such series are really rather fraudulent or, at least, misleading. They are no more than collections of fossils drawn from many different sources and places, often arranged not in chronological order, but according to size.[26] There is no proof whatsoever of any 'family' connection between the specimens, which may even come from different continents. It is as if someone had arranged a random group of birds in order of size and claimed that by this means they had proved the evolution of the wren to the ostrich!

If the theory of evolution is true, it is very surprising that no evidence of a definite common ancestor has yet been discovered in the fossil record of any two different creatures—what we may call a 'missing link'. It is not enough to point out the difference between various *kinds* of horses or apes, for these were already horses and apes. Evidence is needed of some intermediate creature that could have developed into two different things.

Moreover, it is vitally necessary that people who believe in the mutability of species should also make a detailed study of genetics in order to try to work out *how* one creature could possibly evolve into another. Gregor Mendel (1822-1884), for example, was a scientist whose work on genetics was available for Darwin to study, and yet Darwin seems not to have taken advantage of this opportunity. It can be seen now that Mendel's work on inherited char-

---

[26]See *Science Newsletter,* Aug. 25, 1951, p. 118.

acteristics and genetic factors renders Darwin's theory unwork-
able.

Take, as an example, Mendel's work on the inherited color of
eyes or skin, or later research on inherited blood-grouping. If a
blue-eyed person marries another blue-eyed person, the two might
reasonably expect to have blue-eyed children. Now, if no brown-
eyed person had ever entered the 'genetic pool' of that family,
that might well be the case, but once a brown-eyed person comes
into the picture, things can never be the same again.

If a brown-eyed person married a blue-eyed one, the offspring
could be either pure blue, pure brown, or a mixture of brown and
blue, in which case they would *look* brown-eyed. When one consid-
ers the millions of sperm that are sent forth toward the female egg
in order to create one single human baby, it is obvious that even if
the numbers of blue-eyed or brown-eyed possibles are equal, they
will not all have equal chances to 'make it' and be conceived.
However, it is not possible to predict without laboratory interfer-
ence what the infant's eye-color will be. Accordingly, it is perfectly
possible for blue-eyed people to choose to marry other blue-eyed
people for generations and then suddenly produce a brown-eyed
child because the gene is there.[27]

Similarly, if a white-skinned person marries a black-skinned
one, it is quite possible to produce an all-white child or an all-
black one, or one that is a mixture of both colors and therefore
appears to be 'brown'. Suppose that this cross-mixing happened
just once in a family, and the white side of it never again intermar-
ried with the black side. What would happen to the subsequent
offspring? Would they all gradually become paler until the black
gene was evolved out? Not at all; the same chances of the different colors would be there all along. It could easily happen that at
some future time, when all had forgotten that the family ancestry
had ever included a black contributor and all the existing members of the family were as white as they could possibly be, a completely black child could be produced, or vice-versa.

Interestingly enough, the prophet Muhammad (pbuh) was
aware of genetics. He was once approached by an Arab who was
upset because his wife had unexpectedly given birth to a dark

---

[27]For an interesting discussion, see *Evolution, Genetics and Man*, T.
Dobzhansky, NY, John Wiley and Sons, 1955.

child, whereupon Allah's Apostle asked whether the man had any camels. He replied that he did. The Prophet asked about the color, and the man said they were red. The Prophet then asked whether there was a dusky one among them, and the man affirmed that. When asked how this had happened, the man responded that it was perhaps the strain to which it had reverted. The Prophet replied that it is perhaps a strain to which he (the child) has reverted (Muslim).

There exists a major problem in trying to explain the basic mechanism of how one type of living thing could have 'evolved' into another type. This is usually brushed aside by claiming various changes in the nuclei of cells, especially 'accidental' changes known as mutations (mutations are claimed to be the 'raw materials' for evolution).[28]

In fact, the reproduction of genetic material is remarkably accurate, with misprints or miscopying of the DNA occurring very rarely. When such misprints do occur, they are virtually always inferior, harmful or lethal. In other words, they are not good news for the individual carrying the mutant gene. Just in itself, the fact that most mutations are damaging to an organism makes it very difficult to agree that mutation must be the source of the raw materials for evolution; mutants are generally freaks and monstrosities, and when mutants are placed in competition with the normal strain, after one or only a few generations they are eliminated. And in any case, all these mutant possibilities produce variety only within a given species, but never produce a new species.

All these considerations must make an honest evolutionist pause to think. Darwin himself, toward the end of his life, wrote a letter in which he stated that 'the belief in natural selection must at present be grounded entirely on general considerations...when we descend to details...we cannot prove that a single species has

---

[28]See *The New You and Heredity*, Amran Scheinfeld, 1950, p. 476.

changed, nor can we prove that the supposed changes are benefi-
cial, which is the groundwork of the theory'.[29]

---

[29]Letter from Charles Darwin to G. Bentham, written at Down, May
22 (1863), *The Life and Letters of Charles Darwin*, edited by his son, Francis
Darwin, vol.3, John Murray, 1888, p. 25.

It is interesting to note that in his later writing, Wallace also had second thoughts. He claimed that natural selection could not account for
the higher faculties of humanity: 'Natural selection could have
endowed savage man with a brain only a little superior to that of an ape,
whereas he actually possesses one very little inferior to that of a philosopher.' See *Contribution to the Theory of Natural Selection*, A.R. Wallace, 2nd
ed., NY, Macmillan, 1871, p. 356. See also *Issues in Science & Religion*,
I.Barbour, SCM, 1966, p. 92.

CHAPTER ELEVEN

MISSING LINKS

One of the creatures often used by biologists to illustrate evolution is the peppered moth, *biston betularia.* This moth can be either white, white with black spots or stripes, or dark-colored. Before the industrial revolution in England, the light-colored ones were inconspicuous and survived in large numbers in towns, whereas the dark-colored ones tended to be picked off by birds. By 1895, however, about ninety-five percent of the moths in Manchester were dark ones, and the light ones were being picked off. The reason for this was the industrial fumes which blackened the faces of all the city's buildings and walls, thus giving the dark moths the advantage for survival, since the white and speckled ones could now be seen easily by birds. Evolutionists, unaware of what was happening, triumphantly claimed to have had a living example of survival of the fittest by natural selection worked out in front of their very eyes.

Eventually there was not a known surviving white or speckled moth anywhere, and it was assumed that they had died out, the species having now completely evolved into the darker form. Then the city was treated to an expensive clean-up of its imposing stone-work, and suddenly, to the chagrin of these Darwinists, white and speckled moths were everywhere and the black ones were again threatened. Natural selection had not caused the evolution of this moth into the black moth after all; like the genes in Mendel's study of blue and brown eyes, both kinds were still being bred and produced, and it was only the color of the buildings that caused the apparent 'extinction' of the paler forms.

Another fascinating creature much vaunted by evolutionists is

the fruit fly, *drosophila melanogaster*. These are sexually highly
active little creatures which can be bred very swiftly in controlled
conditions, thus producing many generations of successors for
experimenters to examine. Ever since the early 1900s, scientists
eagerly began to subject the poor flies to all sorts of influences—
heat, light, poisons, radiation, anything that might serve as a cata-
lyst to an evolutionary process that could be observed under laboratory conditions.[30] Nothing at all seemed to work on them until
they tried bombarding them with x-rays. Then, all of a sudden,
numerous mutations could be observed.

To the dismay of the researchers, however, all the drosophila
species, although they became more or less hairy, or had mal-
formed wings, legs and bodies, and other distortions, always
remained fruit-flies; there was no sign whatsoever of evolution into
another species as the result of their x-ray treatment. Moreover,
the researchers discovered that the mutated flies were almost without exception inferior to the originals in viability, fertility and
longevity—three highly important factors.[31] The scientists also
found that they could mutate the species only up to a certain
point, at which point the fly became sterile and could no longer
reproduce. That limit is now known as the Hayflick Limit, and it
has been observed for all the other species for which similar
experimentation has taken place. The Hayflick Limit for each
species is not necessarily the same, but the mutated forms always
reach a stage at which they become sterile.

When the mutant flies were left alone to breed without inter-
ference, after some generations even these mutants began to give
birth to normal offspring again, indicating that, had they been left
in their natural state, the normal ones would certainly have been
the survivors over the weaker mutants, preserving the fly in the
form in which it had originally existed. Obviously, DNA, the
hereditary code, has enzymes with an amazing ability to repair
genetic damage.

---

[30]The work of T.H. Morgan (1866-1945) at Columbia University.
Others continued his work, and H.J. Muller received the Noble Prize in
1946 for his contributions in this field.

[31]H.J. Muller commented: 'Most mutations are bad; in fact good
ones are so rare that we may consider them all as bad!' *Time*, November
11, 1946, p. 96. See also *Genetics and the Origin of Species*, T. Dobzhansky,
1951.

When we consider the implications of this, it does not seem to back up the theory of evolution at all. Firstly, it was extremely difficult to produce any genetic mutations whatsoever, and the only influence that had any effect was that of x-rays. Therefore, while evolutionists might like to argue from this that it was a blast of cosmic rays that caused mutations on earth, resulting in one mutated creature whose characteristics were slightly better adapted to the environment than all the rest, thus allowing it to swiftly sweep the board of all its competition, that is impossible to prove.

Secondly, contrary to evolutionary principles, there seems to always be a limit beyond which no further change is possible—and this is always at a stage when the individual creature is still recognizable as *that* creature and has not even begun to develop into anything else.

Also, it seems that the more specialized the breed, the less fit it becomes to survive under natural conditions. It requires an environment artificially free from natural enemies and having artificially abundant and regulated food supplies. Most mutations that have been seen to occur in nature are considerably at risk from their natural environment and are soon weeded out by the mainstream varieties.

There seems to be a biogenic law that life comes only from pre-existing life, and that the parent and its offspring are always of the same 'kind'. It is now possible to make changes in species by artificial selection. One can see walking down a city street numerous different breeds of dogs, for example, from the diminutive Chihuahua to the mighty Great Dane. There are dalmatians, poodles, corgis, Alsatians, dachshunds, bulldogs, and so forth. But they are all dogs, and none of them shows the least sign of becoming anything else. Commercial breeders know very well that after a few generations, an optimum is reached in what they are trying to develop, beyond which further improvement is impossible—moreover, no new species has been formed by their efforts.

And *all* these breeds are quite artificial, man-made. If you were to take a selection of them and lock them all up together for a year or so, the resulting offspring would soon prove what happens to artificial creations when the guards are taken off, for there would be no 'breeds' left at all, but mongrels gradually going back to the original prototype that we could call only 'dog'.

Could different species have arisen as a result of creatures of different species interbreeding? Possibly, but does this happen in nature? You can take a horse and a zebra and produce a hybrid, or a lion and tiger, or a sheep and a goat, or a horse and a donkey—but these are all artificial matings. Left to themselves, these creatures would not mate with each other.

And even the various ape-like species do not interbreed, no matter how much the evolutionists would like them to in order to prove their theories. Monkeys, gorillas, chimpanzees, orangutans, gibbons—all are quite separate species and show no inclination whatsoever to breed together in order to create new species of each other, let alone of man.

So, with nothing to go on that can be observed today, even in the most technologically advanced laboratories, the fossil record becomes the most important evidence for evolution. If the theory were correct, one would expect to find fossils revealing the beginnings of new structures in living things and the slow change from one life form into another.

In fact, the fossil record actually reveals an explosive appearance of highly complex forms of life without any evidence of types in transition, which then all proceeded to reproduce 'after their own kind'. At their very earliest appearance, the major creatures without backbones, for example, were as distinctly set apart as they are today. The transition from invertebrate to vertebrate was supposed to have taken about one hundred million years, but yet there are no fossilized transitional forms whatsoever. Darwin was aware of and embarrassed by all the gaps in the fossil record just at those points where he had hoped to find evidence of transitional forms, and he believed that this would soon be put right by more excavation and research. But was he right? All honest paleontologists have to admit that this has not proved to be the case. The evidence shows that basic kinds of living things appeared suddenly, and, once in existence, did not subsequently change over vast periods of time. Moreover, no transitional linking creatures were discovered.[32]

It has been claimed that archaeopteryx was a transitional form between reptile and bird, but since it had wings and feathers and flew, it *was* a bird! The so-called 'living fossil,' the newly-discovered coelacanth, whose ancestor's skeleton had been found in ancient rocks and whose living descendant has now been fished

---

[32]For an interesting discussion, see *The Fossils Say No*, D.T. Gish.

out of the sea, may have been ugly and the possessor of unusual features, but no one would say it was not a fish. Moreover, the 'modern' coelacanth is identical to the fossils of its predecessors of all those millennia ago; it has not evolved into anything else, so it is patently *not* a transitional anything!

The insect world provides examples of hundreds of possible life cycles. The dragonfly, for example, is a creature that already existed in the Carboniferous period when the coal seams were being laid down—a time during which, as far as is known, not even reptiles lived and the great amphibians were the bulkiest beasts to be seen on land. Now, dragonflies have a most extraordinary life cycle. They start off as eggs laid at the bottom of a pond, and when they hatch, they are rather misleadingly called 'nymphs'—small, grey-brown carnivorous creatures creeping about in the sludge of the pond. When fully-grown, they climb up into the daylight on the stalks of plants, where their bodies become dry. After a time, these nymphs appear to die, but they are actually far from dead, for the nymphs' bodies suddenly split open and perfect dragonflies emerge. And when their wings are dry, they take to the air, leaving their old, cast-off bodies still clinging to the plants.

Dragonflies have been on earth some two hundred million years or so. If the theory of evolution is correct, there must have been aeons prior to the completion of their perfected model when they were 'imperfect' designs, one among many, all struggling against the other, 'contestants' for a time, until, being the fittest of their kind, they completed their evolution and have held their place ever since.

Now, are we to suppose that underwater life was so unpleasant for the nymphs that they pushed themselves up the stalks of giant mare's tails and, by some inexplicable miracle, grew four efficient wings and never returned to the swamps again, except to lay eggs? Are we to imagine countless generations of imperfect nymphs with not-completely-perfect wings clinging fearfully to their plant stems, trying to work out how they might fly? This is obvious nonsense, and so is the thought that the chromosomes in the cells of the insects' shoulders suddenly thought up the possibility of flight and developed wings. There seems to be only one possible explanation: the life cycle of the dragonfly must have been thought out before they were dragonflies, the 'blueprints' already drawn and the insects 'built' according to this plan.

All of the fossils in the geological record appear fully-formed. The picture of life gradually crawling out of the sea or primeval slime to engage in millions of years of bloody war, until the species we see today were forced into their present shapes in the struggle, does not seem to have any foundation in reality. It is an explanation cooked up to fit a theory, and not a theory based upon the whole body of evidence and observed fact. For example, the rocks reveal only bacteria and single-cell plants until around a billion years ago. Then, at the start of the Cambrian period, there was a sudden 'explosion' of fully-developed and highly-complex sea creatures, some now-extinct trilobites actually having more complex and efficient eyes than any currently living arthropod! Below the Cambrian rocks are vast layers of sediments which should have revealed their developing ancestors, but these older beds are virtually barren.[33]

In the layers above the Cambrian, the same 'explosions' of life are repeated, with new kinds of plants and animals being revealed suddenly, without connection to what went before. Moreover, the fossil record goes on to show that these new forms then undergo virtually no subsequent evolution before they become extinct again, which is surely surprising if evolution is the norm for the progress of life. The dragonfly we have now is virtually unchanged from the one that existed forty million years ago.

Evolution within the genetic possibilities of a creature, however, is an observed fact; there clearly *is* an orderly succession of forms of life, changing from the simple to the very complex. The fossil record seems to demonstrate this, for the older the fossil, the less complex the structure. However, although we might consider the structure of fossil bacteria as being 'simple' if compared with the structure of a horse, its biochemical complexity is nevertheless considerable.

---

[33]Darwin himself commented: 'Why, if species have descended from other species by fine gradations, do we not everywhere see innumerable transitional forms? ... Why do we not find them embedded in countless numbers in the crust of the earth? Geological research ... does not yield the infinitely many fine gradations between past and present species required.' (*The Origin of Species*, pp. 178,179, 503). See also *Genetics, Palaeontology and Evolution*, edited by Glenn L. Jepsen, Ernest Mayr, George Gaylord Simpson, 1963, chapter by A.S. Romer, p. 114.

The evolutionary successions in nature seem to be the result of 'mental' activity on the part of a Mind, the life-cycles looking rather like a consequence of this activity producing definite patterns and working according to a fixed plan. There does not seem to be any place in all this for random or chance development. E.C. Kornfield wrote:

> So highly intricate are the organic bio-chemical processes in the animal organism that ... one is rather amazed that a mechanism of such intricacy could ever function properly at all. It demands a planner and sustainer of infinite intelligence. The simplest man-made mechanism requires a planner and a maker. How a mechanism ten thousand times more involved and intricate can be conceived of as self-constructed and self-developed is completely beyond me. [34]

Widening our line of thought a little, some people maintain that they cannot believe in a life after death because the brain disintegrates at death along with the body. But what was it that happened to the dragonfly? Did it not undergo a kind of death and reappear in a new element, in an entirely different form? Just as the nymph may not have had the least inkling that there was a flying insect 'inside' itself to appear when the program deemed it fitting, so the human being cannot imagine the new life form in the Hereafter.

Hence people of faith should be very careful not to ally themselves too closely with any unproven theory, claiming it to be the truth; for if a theory is true, it will continually gather new evidence, rather like a rolling snowball, and scraps of new knowledge will come to it from all sorts of unexpected sources. Everything will fit. If the theory is wrong, however, all sorts of obstacles will crop up, and this is clearly what is happening with Darwinism. The more people struggle to find out how it works, the further away they seem to be from a solution. The obvious possibility that the theory itself is wrong does not seem to occur to many people, since they have been so thoroughly drilled into accepting it since

---

[34] *The Evidence of God in an Expanding Universe,* edited by John Clover Monsma, 1958, p. 176.

childhood. Yet it is not a fact, but simply a working hypothesis, and one which does not seem to work.

There is no clue, for example, to indicate how mammals came from reptiles, if indeed they did, or how birds turned their scales into feathers. There were flying reptiles, to be sure, but there is nothing to indicate that they were ever related to birds. There are no half-way fishes becoming newts, or cold-blooded scaly lizards becoming hairy mammals, no matter how long a period of time we allow for the process. And although evolutionists claim that thousands of thousands of little mutations produced the changes slowly over hundreds of millions of years, the fossil record shows no evidence of this whatsoever.

Millions of bones have been unearthed by evolutionists eager to prove their theories, so there should surely be ample evidence by now to show one kind of living thing evolving into another. In fact, just as Darwin himself was embarrassed by the actual fossil record, which did not show what he predicted it would, so even now, after more than a century of collecting fossils, there are even fewer supposed examples of transitional forms than there were in his day, simply because some of the examples that were used then are now known to be invalid.

Scientists who are prepared to be honest admit that the fossil record does not show transitional forms at all, and that there is no evidence for the gradual development of one life form into another. Rather, the fossil record shows enormous outbursts of fully-formed creatures, evolutionary *leaps*, and it does this at every supposed important transitional stage.

The only way to save face is to assume that new species must have been produced by sudden drastic changes in genetic material—the very *opposite* of what evolutionists actually accept. Anyhow, whichever view is held, there should be some evidence to show one life form turning into another, and there is not. Moreover, there are two further problems: the object of genetic law seems to be to stabilize those mechanisms whose main function is to *prevent* new forms from evolving, and a random step-by-step mutation theory at the molecular level does not explain the organized and growing complexity of life. A theory with just as much right to be heard is that of a Creative Mind.

Now, the earliest known mammals were undistinguished little things that ran around contemporaneously with the last phases of the great lizards. Were these really the ancestors of all mammals, and hence of humans, also? It is hard to believe that a whale, a bat, an elephant and a gorilla are all derived from one parent stock, even though it is a fact that the arm of a man or an ape, the leg of a dog, the flipper of a whale and the wing of a bat are all built on the same skeletal pattern. But it is perfectly easy to grasp that they could have all been evolved from one original concept of mammalness, deliberately determined by an external Mind who arranged the chromosomes at will in the cells of embryos to fit plans already ordained.

Evolutionists usually believe in an orderly succession of development, starting with the formless amoeba and ending up with man; family trees are drawn up, with branches coming out from the parent stem, a tidy and convincing picture. It is also commonly held that if living tissue were reduced to its minutest components, we would eventually discover what life actually is and be able to produce living organisms. But there is another factor. Even if the 'germ of life' could be found, one would not be able to make that germ develop without adding thought to it. Life is always a compound of its chemical constituents and mind itself— and one cannot take mind to pieces and examine it under a microscope.

And as far as the fossil record of man is concerned, it is extraordinarily suspect. Since the living world does not provide any link whatsoever between human beings and the ape family, fossil evidence becomes vital if one wishes to prove this link.[35] It should strike everyone as quite odd that, if humans are really no more than better-developed apes, the so-called 'inferior' versions are still in existence, and not a single one of them in an intermediary form between human and ape. It is surely very odd, likewise, that the old originals are still around, while all the intermediate links which led to the full-fledged human have died out.

After more than a century of earnest searching, every museum and book on evolution presents graphically the development of something in the ape family into ape-men and then into humans, but most of this presentation is nothing more than clever and rather biased imagination, and not based on proven facts.

---

[35] *The Primates,* Sarel Elmerl and Irven de Vore, the editors of *Life,* 1965, p. 15.

After combing the earth, the entire fossil record for the whole story of human evolution could be laid out on one table-top, or packed, with plenty of room to spare, in one coffin! It consists of little more than a handful of teeth and bone fragments, some of which are under dispute and the suspicion of fraud. When monkeys first appeared in the fossil record, they were monkeys, and when humans first appeared, they were human.

Various of the supposed ape-men have been given the names Ramapithecus, Australopithecus, Zinjanthropus, Java Man, Peking Man and Neanderthal Man. Ramapithecus, who lived fourteen million years ago, is known only from a few fragments of jawbones and teeth, and was certainly an ape. Next, although Australopithecus was once overwhelmingly accepted as our ancestor, it is now recognized that although it has human-like teeth, its skull is simian and it is now discounted as a hominid. Zinjanthropus was probably a variety of Australopithecus, and its two subversions, Robustus and Africanus (the latter being the famous skeleton, 'Lucy'), are probably simply the male and female of the same creature. Java Man's remains consist of a skull-cap and three teeth, together with a human leg bone found some distance away. Moreover, there is some suspicion about the circumstances of his discovery.[36]

In the 1920s-1930s, fragments of thirty skulls, eleven lower jaws, and 147 teeth were found, supposedly of Peking Man. All this material disappeared during the period of 1941-45. Piltdown Man, discovered in 1912, was believed for forty years to be genuine, but was found to consist of human bones and an ape's jaw put together and artificially aged.[37] And Nebraska Man's remains consisted of nothing more than one tooth of an extinct pig.[38]

On the other hand, Neanderthal Man, who stood fully erect and had a larger brain capacity than modern man's, was no missing link; he was definitely fully human. Early representations portrayed him as being bent over, stupid-looking, hairy and apelike, but it was then shown that this reconstruction was based on the

---

[36]See, for a discussion of skeletal evidence, *Man, Time and Fossils*, Ruth Moore, Cape, 1954.

[37]See *Science Newsletter*, Feb 25, 1961, p. 119, and *Encyclopedia Britannica*, 1946, vol.14, p. 763.

[38]*The Fossil Evidence for Human Evolution*, W. Le Gros Clark, 1964, pp. 26-27.

fossil skeleton of an individual Neanderthaler who had been badly deformed by disease.[39] The many Neanderthalers found since show that he was not much different from modern humans (the Cro-Magnon hominids were also full-fledged humans).

Humans, like all species, only reproduce 'after their own kind,' and are separate and distinct. Just as with animals, there are plenty of variations within the species, from tiny pygmies to huge seven-footers, with many skin and hair colors, with eyes of various shapes, and so on. But they all belong to the same 'kind,' which is human and not any form of an ape.

So, all in all, it can be said bluntly that the evidence for evolution is by no means conclusive, and we are entitled to keep an open mind on the subject. Darwin's Galapagos finches illustrated variety within a kind, allowed for by a creature's genetic make-up. The finches were still finches, and not transforming into anything else. If they are honest, future scientists may well be amazed and amused by the way the wild theories of evolution so easily captivated twentieth-century minds and were so widely and recklessly applied.

---

[39] *The World Book Encyclopedia*, 1966, vol.15, p. 672.

CHAPTER TWELVE

THE 'OPEN-SYSTEM' HUMUS CHAIN

Now, having hinted that the things our senses tell us are extremely limited, if not actually inaccurate or incomplete, and that most of our ideas about the world in which we live are misleading, can we arrive at any answer to the question, 'Who am I?'

At this point it seems reasonable to say that I know virtually nothing about this world. But of one thing I am quite sure, and that is that I really do exist. But, as usual, 'I' can mean all sorts of things.

Firstly, as we have seen, on the physical level 'I' consists of a collection of atoms. Every single part of my body consists of atoms, and as long as 'I' exist as a person, those atoms seem to want to continue to be a part of me. Biologists tell us that we change every single atom in our bodies every seven years or so; and yet, no matter how much we have grown, slimmed, aged, or changed in any other way, we still feel that we are the 'same' person.

Isn't it fascinating to go over old family photographs and trace the bodily changes of a particular person (perhaps yourself) over the years? We all think so. And while the changes can be enormous, at no point do individuals feel that they are becoming different persons.

The next extraordinary thing to contemplate is the strange way in which our physical bodies don't really belong to us as fixed entities at all; they are no more than a continuous interchange of atoms with the atomic material around us. They constitute what are known as 'open systems'. If we sealed up our bodies so that nothing whatsoever could go in or out of them, they would become 'closed systems,' and we would die in a matter of seconds.

'I' as an entity am kept alive by several marvelous open processes or systems. One of these systems is that of the provision of food for myself, and this involves an interaction with the whole of nature. We know, to take one simple example, that the body needs calcium; it gets this largely from milk or from products made from milk.[40] However, the matter is even more complicated in reality, because we usually get our milk by inducing other animals to have babies, and then drinking the milk intended for their offspring!

The body needs also iron and many other minerals such as phosphorus, iodine, sulphur and potassium, but it cannot get these by simply eating a spoonful of minerals or chewing on a bar; in fact, if we swallowed a mouthful of phosphorus or potassium, it would probably kill us! But the body manages to get what it needs by eating plants that have already absorbed these minerals into themselves, which are then presented to us in a digestible, assimilable form. Who would have thought it? We get our iron by eating a cabbage!

Similarly, the body needs proteins, and it gets these mainly by eating meat—in other words, the flesh of slaughtered animals and other animal products.

Without this continuous supply of material passing into us from the life forms around us, we would soon die—and, of course, if they were not absorbing material from other living things, so would they. The fascinating thing about matter is that it seems to go round and round forever, passing through all sorts of bodies in an endless 'chain'.

Even more fascinating is the discovery that once a piece of matter has become 'alive,' it then continues to stay alive and cannot go back to being 'dead' matter. And the easy way to convert a piece of dead matter (such as a molecule of iron) into living matter is simply to eat it. Once dead matter enters a digestive system, it gets broken down, passes into the bloodstream, and gets utilized by the living entity by becoming part of that entity's 'body'.

Even if it was later evacuated as a waste product, it would not be able to go back to being 'dead' matter, for our bodily wastes

---

[40]In countries where there are virtually no dairy products in the diet after infancy (i.e. Southeast Asia), calcium is obtained from green leafy vegetables or sea vegetables.

find their way back to the soil and help to build up the supply of humus, the food supply of green plants. Life feeds on life, and once caught up in the network of living matter, atoms remain 'living' through countless life cycles that may last for thousands of years. Evolution seems to have moved from totally dead inorganic matter to everlasting self-replicating life in one swift step.

Where does the chain begin? That's like asking the old question, 'Which came first, the chicken or the egg?' The whole process is an unending circle. Even our bodies are the food of other organisms; germs live on us while we are alive, and microbes soon break down our corpses and dispose of them when we die. Sometimes these microscopic organisms cause us great distress, when our bodies become 'dis-eased,' but at other times they pass cheerfully through our skin or eyeballs or nostrils or blood vessels without disturbing us in any way. They are quite at home.

Another of our marvelous systems is that of the flow of gases through us. Apart from things we recognize as 'food,' our bodies also need a continuous supply of oxygen, and they accumulate carbon dioxide as a waste product. And yet another amazing thing is that a large proportion of our bodies is made of water. Now, have you ever stopped to think that water, a liquid, is simply the 'miraculous' result of joining one molecule of oxygen, a colorless gas, to two molecules of hydrogen, another colorless gas?

Our lungs enable us to suck in air, a complicated mixture of various gases, extract the one we need, and, when breathing out, to get rid of whatever we don't need. This is why people die of suffocation when sealed in an airtight space; they use up all the oxygen in the air shut in with them, changing it all into something they cannot breathe.

When you think about it, this is quite alarming, for perhaps there could come a time when all the breathing creatures on earth would have sucked up all the available air and used up all the oxygen. Then what? Will they, and we, all die? Well, we might, were it not for the amazing fact that the green leaves of plants also breathe, but they do things in reverse. They breathe in carbon dioxide and breathe out oxygen; so, as long as we don't destroy the balance provided by the earth's trees and green plants, living creatures will still have air to breathe. This, of course, is the main reason why ecologists get so upset about the cutting down of a rain forest the size of Kansas each year, for these great forests are the main suppliers of the earth's oxygen.

Did you ever stop to consider what an important symbol the names of the first man and woman are? The Latin word for the living part of the soil is '*humus*'. The Old Testament scriptures, in which the names of the first man and woman were first recorded, were written in Hebrew, and the Hebrew word for the same thing is *adamah*. So, the Latin word for a *humus*, or mud-creature, or earthling, is 'human,' and the Hebrew word for human is 'Adam'. 'Eve' ('Hawwah' in Arabic) means 'breath' or 'living soul'.

Think about the actual physical content of a human body as it grows and develops from infancy to adulthood. The weight of a baby at its moment of birth is around five to eight pounds. As it grows up, it will take into itself matter from the things living and growing around it until it weighs around 150 pounds—and all that extra material once belonged to the 'landscape'. Dieters experience the reverse; they shed off numerous pounds of their bodies back into the 'landscape,' or 'bank of living matter'.

However, our bodies, fantastic and complicated though they are, are not really our 'selves'. They are only the physical agglomeration of atoms that belong to us for a limited time, and even then, they are changing all the time and interacting with the environment, the 'bank of matter'.

These physical atoms of matter are moving around and changing from one form into another, passing without your being aware of it 'through' the body you think you own. It's quite comical to suppose that you could absorb a geranium into your own body simply by eating it, and equally, that you could be absorbed by a geranium by being buried under its roots. Every life form shares this bank of matter, and the stuff of which things are made never ceases to exist; it merely 'flows' from one thing to another.

Living matter differs from dead matter in that it is very much more organized and complicated. Living things are made of very ordinary atoms, but they are ones which have the special characteristic of joining together in large bunches. Most atoms simply do not do this; for example, hydrogen and oxygen will combine in several forms, but none of them contains more than four atoms. If nitrogen is added, there are more possible combinations, but not a great many more. When carbon is added, however, those original gases will suddenly combine to form molecules with thousands of atoms in them. In some mysterious way, carbon seems to be the key to all living things.[41]

Life can exist only under suitable conditions of light, heat and radiation. The universe as a whole was clearly not designed just for the purpose of supporting 'life,' since so much of it, and the vast majority of its laws, are totally against the existence of life. Yet life *does* exist, in spite of enormous odds, and, on our planet at least, it thrives.

Living things are made up of atoms that have become cells, and when observed under a microscope, each of these cells appears to be quite independent of those around it. Each one— and an average adult's body contains some 350 billion of them— seems to eat, rest, grow, work, reproduce, and die all by itself.

Probably the most fascinating question is how a living structure as complicated as a human being comes into existence. A single fertilized living cell divides, again and yet again, until the original 'egg-cell' has become about twenty-six million million cells, the average number in a newborn baby's body. In all those millions of individual little units, each cell has taken up its correct position. Each cell has assumed the required size and shape and is located in the right place, to enable it to perform a specific function—as part of a limb, a muscle, a nerve, an organ. And it has done all this as if it knew what it was supposed to do, as if it had gradually been following a definite plan or design.[42]

Each minute part of the whole is perfectly fitted for its environment and for the task it will have to perform; this has been well-documented by the modern equipment at our disposal.[43] In one scientific program, data about the function and performance of a blood cell were fed into a computer, yielding all the information about what the cell would have to do, the speeds at which it would have to travel, and so on. The response, for which the computer was programmed, consisted of a diagram (which was quickly produced by the computer) of the most perfect shape the blood

---

[41]*Romeo Error,* Lyall Watson, 1974, p. 21.

[42]*Life,* April 30, 1965, pp. 70,72A.

[43]This was also suggested by the writer of the Psalm 139: 'Thou (God) didst see my limbs unformed in the womb, and in Thy book they are all recorded: day by day they were fashioned, and not one of them was late in developing' verse 16.

cell could possibly have in order to best fulfill all its functions. The investigator then pricked his thumb and squeezed out a drop of blood, which he examined under a microscope. Needless to say, it was of exactly the shape recommended by the computer![44]

Now, the important question is—did the blood cell evolve gradually until it attained its present characteristics? If so, how was it that evolution had stopped precisely at the point when the most perfect shape was reached? Why would it have stopped evolving? If it had been possible to carry out the same experiment millennia earlier, would a computer have revealed that the blood cell was not yet perfected for its task?

There is no way of knowing, but it seems extremely unlikely. From what *is* known about our universe, it appears that everything is already perfect and exactly fulfills the functions set for it *at every stage of life.*

Those who argue strongly for a process of trial and error over millennia, or the chance takeover of some superior gene, are not being realistic. If any minutest cell or particle were not already completely adapted for its task, it would not survive at all.

Another interesting and rather uncomfortable thought is that life depends on death. The cells on the exterior of our bodies begin to produce fibrous keratin until the whole cell body is filled with the substance, and then they technically die. Isn't it odd to think that our living bodies are covered in a dead layer which is continually being shed and replaced by more living cells coming from within and dying?

Inside us, there are whole armies of cells that 'lay down their lives' to preserve us as one living organism. For every thousand red cells in our blood, there are white ones that creep along the walls of the blood vessels, ready for instant action when the body is under threat. They congregate rapidly at sites of infection or wounds, absorb particles of pollution in the lungs, dissolve splinters, and generally attack anything foreign to the system; they also take intrusive bacteria captive by flowing around them. As many as twenty bacteria can be imprisoned and digested within a single white cell, but these cells frequently die from the effects of the bacterial toxins, and the pus which appears at the site of the conflict is the accumulation of these dead white cells. To have too few

---

[44] *The River of Life*, Rutherford Platt, 1956.

white cells would be disastrous for us, but an overproduction of them results in leukemia.

Under normal circumstances, a perfect balance is maintained; each day some parts of us die so that the rest of us can live. These deaths are not due to chance or to a competition leading to the survival of the fittest. This death is programmed into life; a living organism cannot survive unless the death of various bits of it happens on schedule.[45]

Furthermore, if death did not exist, the fastest breeders would soon take over the world, for one bacterium can reproduce itself and build up a mass equivalent to the weight of an average man in a few hours. It is startling to realize that each ounce of soil contains around a hundred million bacteria; unchecked, bacteria would cover the entire surface of the earth in two days. Incidentally, no bacteria reach death from old age—they simply reach optimum size and then divide.

Perhaps the most fascinating thought of all is to contemplate the origin of sex. In the 1940s, Joshua Lederberg of Columbia University was able to demonstrate that some cells of the common colon bacillus did not just go on dividing forever, but began to exist in two forms—male and female—and that they began to transmit hereditary material between intact individuals in a process of injection that can only be described as 'sexual'.[46] Once cells could be described as either male or female, and multiplied by interchanging small parts of their bodies in a union that produced new individuals, there came into existence for the first time what could properly be described as life cycles. The cells did not just divide, but developed, grew old and died. It was now possible to differentiate between 'immortal' cells, which just kept on and on dividing, and those which lived as specific individuals.

Of course, there is always a price to pay, and the price which living matter pays for sex and for individuality is death.

---

[45]See *Romeo Error*, Lyall Watson, Hodder and Stoughton, 1974, p. 24.
[46]Ibid., p. 29.

CHAPTER THIRTEEN

THE GHOST IN THE MACHINE

Now here's another strange thought. Supposing that you were simply one of these cells in your own body, you would see things from a very different point of view than your 'self's' present perspective. You would see vast spaces all around yourself, and you would be looking for food and avoiding attack by germs. An interesting question is: Does the individual cell know that *you* exist?

Another strange thing is that, although the actual atoms in our bodies change all the time, I still feel that 'I' am 'me,' even though my body may shrink or expand or age. Then surely somewhere inside my mortal frame is a 'person' or 'being' that remains the same despite any physical changes; certainly I'm not aware of having become anyone else. Could it be that 'I' am the 'pattern,' and that 'I' go on controlling my atomic structure throughout my lifespan? Is my material body, with all its workings, inexorably governed by natural law, and just a machine, or is there really a 'ghost' in my machine?

Suppose I buy an old car and drive it around until the wheels burst, and then replace the wheels; and when the engine fails, replace the engine; and when the chassis rusts away, replace the chassis; and whenever any part goes wrong, replace that. Now, after I've driven it for a million miles, am I still driving the same car? Is my body not exactly like that car, continually having every little bit replaced and renewed, and yet still being 'me'?

Conscious beings are intuitively aware that there is more to the human being than the material 'bag of tricks'. We are more than simply the products of nature, wonderful machines obeying the laws of the universe though our bodies are. It's an unquestionable truth that our physical bodies come into being, stock themselves up, keep themselves going for a time, and finally run down and disintegrate. But there is something else about us. There is a 'driver' in our 'machine'. 'I' am not simply an entity occupying a set of atoms for a particular time.

Let's think about this concept of 'I' for a moment. When I think about my 'self,' I don't usually mean it as a reference to my mechanical and physical processes, all those things going on inside me that I'm normally not aware of at all. But there is an 'I' who gets angry when people irritate me, an 'I' who gets hurt when I find out that people don't like me, an 'I' who falls in love and desperately wants to be loved in return. 'I' get frightened and am either hopeful about things or in despair. And when 'I' have a pain in my stomach or my leg, 'I' feel it's something that is *happening to* me, not that it *is* me. I am aware of a difference between my 'self' and my body.

Maddeningly, I cannot prove scientifically that 'I' exist at all. 'I' am quite sure that I do exist, and I am aware of the fact that I can think. But some materialist scholars insist that thinking and memory and awareness of personality are all just functions of the brain, which can be 'set up' by stimulating certain areas of it. A 'mind' or 'soul' cannot be extracted during an operation and examined. It cannot be seen at all; therefore, according to such thinkers, it doesn't exist. Or does it?

Maybe we have more than one self. There is the Me I know and am conscious of. Then there is the Nasty Me whom I try to control but who 'makes' me do things I know I shouldn't be doing. Third, there is the Ideal Standard Me whom I know I could be if I tried hard enough. And finally, there is the Very Highest Me who is of an ideal standard of righteousness that I know I could never reach but am still able to contemplate.

Christians, Muslims and Jews all believe that people possess one soul. Hindus also say that we have one, but that it keeps coming around again from existence to existence. The ancient Egyptians claimed that we have at least five. Many modern psychologists say that we have none, but acknowledge that we have 'sides' to our characters with strange names like ego, id, and superego.

Yet if the soul does not exist, it is strange indeed that a belief in it has been virtually universal throughout all recorded history. If a thing does not exist and never has, is it really possible to conceive of it at all? What gave people the crazy idea that they had souls in the first place?

The study of thought is of fundamental importance. Thought is the force by which mind operates; enlarge your thinking and you extend your mind. Don't do so, or rely on the products of other people's thinking, and you are more useless than a slug creeping along on the surface of the earth.

Can we really be certain, as materialist philosophers and scientists would have us be, that the human being is no more than a kind of glorified machine, a being that reacts 'mechanically,' having been programmed by emotions, environment, or biochemical processes? Or could it rather be true that the person is not the body at all, but the soul who inhabits that body for a given time? And if we really are souls, rather than merely being bodies, then the materialistic conclusions of atheist scientists are extremely false, misleading representations of the true nature of the human being.

Many people claim to have experienced what are now termed 'out-of-body' or 'near-death' experiences, during which, they believe, they have had the quite extraordinary experience of their awareness being extended beyond their own bodies for some reason (usually at the time of an accident or heart attack, or during surgery), and they believe they were then able to look down on their vacated physical selves from some vantage point in the room, perhaps near the ceiling of the room in which they had 'died'.

Here's an example reported by a perfectly down-to-earth and intelligent medical officer attached to the Royal Flying Corps, taken from the *Journal of the Society for Psychical Research* 39: 692,1957.[47] The officer crashed his plane on takeoff at a small country airfield and was thrown out of the cockpit. He landed on his back in a hollow in the ground, where none of the airfield buildings were visible. When help arrived, he was completely unconscious. Yet he remembered looking down at the scene of the crash from a point of view some two hundred feet above it.

The officer saw his own body, and his brigadier and the uninjured pilot running toward it; he felt slightly irritated that they were interested in it and wished they would leave it alone. He then saw an ambulance start out but stall, and the driver get out to

---

[47]See also *The Romeo Error,* Lyall Watson, Hodder and Stoughton, 1974, p. 140.

use a starting handle. He watched the ambulance call at a hospital, where the orderly collected something, and then eventually they arrived and took him away on a journey. He regained consciousness as they were pouring sal volatile (a restorative similar to smelling salts) down his throat. The ensuing inquiry into the circumstances proved correct in every detail the officer's version of what had taken place while he was supposedly unconscious.

Recent scientific surveys and experiments into 'out-of-body' experiences seem to suggest that there is much more involved here than individuals' merely having visions or hallucinations brought on by shock or oxygen deprivation.

Dr. Peter Fenwick, for example, is the consultant neuropsychiatrist at the Maudsley Hospital in London. He has studied literally hundreds of professed out-of-body or near-death experiences. He was originally interested in the science of consciousness, and is now convinced that souls are able to leave the body and pick up information and see things that the unconscious body would be totally unaware of. He believes that investigation into this phenomenon has now advanced to such a stage that anyone, no matter how skeptical, should be able to accept the possibility that the mind/consciousness/soul can detach itself and leave the brain.

People who believe that they have had such 'near-death' experiences generally find them the most exciting and fascinating thing that has ever happened to them, and as a result, their whole attitude toward life and death, and the importance of life, changes. Such people insist that, from the moment of their experience, they no longer entertain any doubt that the soul is *not* the same thing as some function of the brain, but is the entity that is destined to return to God after our earthly lives, even though our earthly bodies rot away or are disposed of in some other fashion. Whether or not God will choose to resuscitate our physical bodies in some miraculous way becomes almost irrelevant to them, for they are totally convinced that the real person is the soul and not the body it briefly inhabits.

Quite typical of the cases reported is that of student Catherine Norton (reported in *Women's Own* magazine, June 22, 1992), who described what happened to her on the day complications set in after a routine operation. She had her tonsils out and went home from the hospital, but a few days later started hemorrhaging very badly. Her mother rushed her back to the hospital, where she was placed in a side ward.

Suddenly, she reported later, she found herself looking down at her body from the ceiling, seeing the back of her head but unable to see her face. She could observe the doctors attending to her, but felt very peaceful and wanted to be left alone. Catherine stated that the experience was not scary and she didn't feel panicky about dying. She reviewed her short life very happily and thought about what a wonderful time she had had with her family. Then everything went black, and she woke up in bed with an intravenous drip in her arm. Up to this point she had not been given any drugs, and if anything, she thought she might have had the experience because she'd lost so much blood. As she was not religious and did not connect the incident with death, she was able to put a name to what had happened to her only after seeing a television program about near-death experiences.

The vast majority of so-called out-of-body experiences take place at the time of an accident or illness, but they have also been reported by people who have been under the influence of drugs or anaesthetics, and by those who claim to have had such experiences during sleep or drowsiness. There are reports of a few cases of people supposedly projecting their souls beyond their bodies deliberately, at will, usually under procedures involving hypnosis or relaxation techniques adopted during meditation or yoga.

Charles Tart, of the University of California, recently completed a pilot study of Robert Monroe, a subject who claimed to be able to come out of his body at will .[48] Electroencephalographic records taken of him in this state showed that he was neither dreaming nor properly awake, but was producing slow alpha-wave activity while his body was in a state of semi-paralysis.

Although science has not documented the occurrence of metaphysical experiences, we must recognize that it lacks the tools by which to identify or measure such phenomena. When dealing with matters that can neither be proved nor disproved, the most reasonable course is to maintain an open mind.

In the determination of the existence of the soul itself, while we may not be able to find or measure that intangible entity, surely our innermost hearts tell us that we are more than mere machines.

---

[48] *Journeys Out of the Body*, Monroe, R.A., Doubleday, New York, 1971.

CHAPTER FOURTEEN

WHERE DO WE GO FROM HERE?

A belief in the survival of one's person after bodily death has been widespread since the earliest of times. Humans are instinctively aware that they have a 'self,' and they know that a time will inevitably come when their physical bodies will cease to function. So naturally, they are very interested to know what will happen to their 'selves' after that moment of death.

Obviously, if a person's 'self' is nothing more than a part of the brain-center and the atomic construction of the human being, then the 'self,' like the body, will cease to be after the moment of death, breaking down and decomposing just like the rest of the body. If there is no soul, there is no life after death in the sense that a *person* continues to exist. Consequently, the only form of immortality you would be left with would be that of passing on some part of your genetic structure to your children, whose material bodies and programs start off within your body. Most of us would not really regard that as immortality, however; this is not what we have in mind when we contemplate our hoped-for future survival as persons.

If we can accept the notion that a non-material soul inhabits the particular group of atoms belonging to us, despite the many changes taking place all the time in that group, then wouldn't it be possible for our souls to go on existing as separate entities apart from our physical bodies?

The earliest of people thought so, and left either real or symbolic food and drink and various useful objects in the graves of their dead, or set up shrines for them in their old homes, in order that their shades could continue to live happily alongside their families.

The ancient Greeks and Hebrews envisaged a rather gloomy afterlife for their beloved dead. They believed that there was a land for departed spirits somewhere beneath the earth, a miserable and desolate place to which no one would want to go. Naturally, if such was the lot of the 'departed,' then death was indeed to be regretted and feared. It would be far better not to 'survive' at all, but instead to abandon one's self to nothingness, or to a state of eternal sleep. It was probably fearful notions like these that led relatives to pray for their dead loved ones to 'rest in peace' and not be condemned to eternal wandering about in misery as unhappy shades.

Many religious thinkers were not at all happy to think that God could abandon in such an awful place individuals whom He had loved and cared for; it seemed totally unreasonable and out of keeping with thoughts of God as a Supreme Being of Love, who was also in control of everything, including life after death. And some, especially the Jewish Pharisees and early Christians, considered the possibility that the dead entered a state of sleep that would end on a great Day of Resurrection, when God would cause flesh to be miraculously restored to decayed bones and their souls would re-enter their former bodies.

Others believed that after death we would experience not a mere sleep, but our souls' journeying to somewhere else. And this 'somewhere' was not foreordained to be a grim place of dust and darkness, for surely a just God would establish varied consequences for our souls, depending on whether we warranted reward or punishment for our deeds in this life.

It has been suggested, of course, that any kind of belief in the happy survival of the self after death is nothing more than wishful thinking. People naturally don't want to be 'snuffed out' and can't bear the thought that all their work and effort will come to nothing. They also have a strong desire to be reunited with deceased family and friends whom they had dearly loved.

If it could be proved that there was no life after death, a great many people would certainly give up bothering to be religious, since there would be no blessed reward or joyful reunion to come, no longer any point in trying to live a good, unselfish life to attain salvation in the Hereafter. Others might give up out of a sense of despair at the injustice of there being no future time or state in which wrongs would be put right and people compensated or punished for what they had done, frustrated that they obviously are not rewarded or punished during their present lifetime.

Now, while Heaven or Hell may be an extremely obvious fate for the real saints or villains, it surely does present a problem when it comes to borderline cases. Doesn't this make nonsense out of the whole notion? How will God decide for those of us who are neither very good nor very bad, but somewhere in the middle?

Some believe that though He doesn't consign us to Hell, in order to get into Heaven we will either have to be suddenly very much improved, or else there must be a process of gradual development that will continue after the death of our bodies. Roman Catholic doctrine suggests a place called Purgatory, a state in which souls not yet fit for Heaven might be purified and cleansed. However, other theologians, including many of the Jewish Pharisees at the time of the Blessed Jesus, believed that if our good deeds outweighed our bad ones by even the slightest amount, God would have mercy on us. The Qur'an presents the Day of Judgement as the culmination of God's mercy, when good and evil will finally be sorted out:

> He has inscribed for Himself (the rule of) mercy. There is no doubt whatever that He will gather you together for the Day of Judgement (surah 6:12).

> We shall set up scales of justice for the Day of Judgement, so that not one soul will be dealt with unjustly in the least. And if there be (no more than) the weight of a mustard seed, We will bring it (to account) (surah 21:47).

From the Islamic perspective it is interesting to note here that though good deeds are important, they are not in themselves sufficient for a person's salvation, which depends only on God's grace. The prophet Muhammad (pbuh) is reported to have said, 'None of you will enter Paradise on account of your good deeds alone.' The people asked him, 'Even you, O Prophet of God?' He replied, 'Yes, even me, unless God bestows His favor and mercy on me' (Bukhari).

Belief in the afterlife is the most decisive factor in human life. Acceptance or rejection of it determines the very course of a human being's living patterns and behavior. Even though they may be good, unselfish individuals, people who believe that this world is all there is are obviously only concerned with their success or failure in this world. But those who believe in the afterlife are very well aware that it gives meaning and purpose to earthly life; they live, as it were, with their two feet in two worlds, and thoughts and concerns for the life hereafter provide a very strong motivation in all they do.

The fact that many 'progressive' people doubt the reality of the afterlife is not really due to science. It is the 'logic' of materialism which insists that, since after death a person is reduced to dust and since no person has ever witnessed a case of the revival of a decayed corpse, death and destruction *must* be the end of life and there is nothing after it. But is this truly scientific reasoning? Not to those who acknowledge that there are still unrecognized dimensions of reality. Even if not one single person has ever seen a case of revival, this only means that we can state with certainty that we do not *know* what will happen after death. It does not imply that nothing will happen. Science tells us nothing, either negative or positive, in this respect.

Just because no one has seen a thing does not mean that it has no existence or cannot occur. Honest scientists of real insight teach that there is a very great deal more even to physical existence and the material universe than that which we mortals can perceive with our limited senses. They admit that there may exist a realm which is not accessible to human awareness or bound by the limitations of the human intellect; it is utterly beyond human perception and remains Hidden or Unseen. The known material universe with which we are familiar is like only the tip of an iceberg, the bulk of which remains hidden from our eyes. Consequently, it should be admitted that the universe is full of all sorts of things that human beings have never seen and cannot imagine; the continued existence of the human soul after the death of the body is not a matter that any person is in a position to categorically deny.

All people will unquestionably 'taste' death. If they have souls, then it is entirely possible that these souls will leave their bodies, while their corpses rot away and their atoms go back to replenish the soil from which they were made.

There may be another life of a very different nature from the life of this world, a life in which we will be so completely transformed that we cannot understand it, no matter how hard we try. Islam, for example, teaches that:

> No person knows what delights of the eye are kept hidden for them, a reward for their (good) deeds (surah 32:17).

> In Paradise I [God] have prepared for the righteous believers what no eye has ever seen, no ear has ever heard, and what the keenest mind could never imagine (Hadith Qudsi).

We can easily point out the fallacy of supposing that restoring already created beings — ourselves — to life is in any way difficult for God. As the Qur'an puts it:

> How can you disbelieve in God when you were dead and He gave you life? Then He will cause you to die and then will again bring you to life. Then to Him you will return (surah 2:28).

> Is not He Who created the heavens and the earth able to create the like thereof?—Yes, indeed! For He is the Creator Supreme, of (infinite) skill and knowledge! (surah 36:81).

> Do humans think that We cannot re-assemble their bones? Nay, We are able to put (them) together in perfect order, (even) their fingerprints (surah 75:3-4).

People who believe in God are therefore obliged to regard 'mechanical' and 'materialistic' interpretations of the universe as actually being irrational, inferior, false and misleading.

CHAPTER FIFTEEN

THINKING ABOUT EVIL

When people believe that there is a God and that He is the Supreme Force for Good, they are faced with the serious problem of the many painful and terrible things happening in our world that seem to be quite irreconcilable with any notion of a benign and compassionate Creator.

Simply expressed, the problem is this: If God really is Supreme, then He must, by definition, be able to do anything and everything. If He is Omniscient, then He must know everything that exists or occurs, down to the minutest details. If He is Omnipotent or All-Powerful, then there cannot be anything that He cannot do. Yet beyond any shadow of doubt, a great deal of suffering and evil exists, often in ways that are beyond our minds to accept. Obviously at least one of the proposed suggestions about God must be wrong.

If He is All-Knowing, then He is certainly aware of human tragedies and awful sufferings; if He is All-Powerful, He could stop and eradicate all our problems if He so wished; if He is All-Loving, He should certainly wish to do so. The fact that evil and suffering exists therefore apparently suggests that either God is *not* All-Powerful and does not have the ability to do anything about evil, or that He is *not* All-Knowing and remains somehow unaware of suffering, or that He is aware of it and could do something about it, but does not do so and is therefore *not* All-Loving.[49]

---

[49]This problem was first expressed by the philosopher Epicurus (341-270 B.C.E.), quoted by Lactantius (260-340 C.E.), and later by St. Augustine (353-430). See *On the Anger of God,* chap. 13, trans. William Fletcher, in *The Writings of the Ante-Nicene Fathers,* Grand Rapids, Michigan, vol. vii, 1951.

One must pause to wonder why it is that suffering and evil exist at all. If God is truly the Creator, why did He create the possibility of such pain and despair and horror? Is there something limited in either God's power or His good intentions, or is there simply no moral aspect at all abroad in the universe, with things just happening as they do because that is the way it is?

Let's take a specific example of human suffering and think about its implications. Suppose there is a child being swept away in a flooded river, drowning because he cannot reach the bank and safety. If a bystander stood there watching with a life-line in his hand but did not throw it to the child when he had the power to do so, we would certainly regard that person as a villain and accuse him of being morally responsible for the child's death.

If you translate this example up to the level of God's watching some poor human being floundering in the mire, you can see precisely why so many people who are obliged to go through some dreadful sufferings from time to time find it hard to believe in a compassionate, caring, and All-Powerful God.

God, who 'sees the smallest sparrow fall,' ought to see the child in distress and do something about it. Most religious people grew up with the belief that God did wondrous deeds for His followers of old, even supplying an occasional miracle when one was needed. Then why doesn't He do it now?

Sometimes, people claim, God *does* influence the outcome of events by interfering with human consciousness. He uses the consciences of individuals, groups, and nations, to make them feel shame at not being active in putting matters aright when people are suffering abuse, maltreatment, or national disasters such as drought and famine or war.

Sometimes God appears to communicate with individuals through some kind of psychic faculty, perhaps sending premonitions or warnings or visions of things that later come to pass. People get uncomfortable feelings or vivid dreams about particular planes or trains, and avoid traveling on them. Then, when the planes or trains crash, they feel their hunches or premonitions were signs of divine intervention. Perhaps they were.

It would certainly be very nice to think that if we prayed hard enough or had lived good enough lives, then, when we got into a tricky situation, God would somehow or other fix things so that we were miraculously saved from whatever it was that was threatening us. But, as we all know only too well, God doesn't operate like that. And, as all ministers of religion know only too well, when people's prayers are not answered and their loved ones drown or die of cancer or crash their cars, all too often the result is that they lose their belief in God, for in their view, if God refuses to help those who have done nothing to 'deserve' suffering, then there is no sense or advantage in belief. To them, all religious fervor and promises of God's love and beneficence look like so many pious wishes, totally unjustified.

Countless philosophical brains have grappled with the problem of suffering, and numerous clever answers have been put forward. On examining these closely, we find that most of these are subjective in nature and reflect the personal biases of their proponents.

God is indeed Supreme, Omnipotent and Omniscient, but are we way off track in supposing that we are in any way special to Him? Out of all the millions of life forms that God has created, why should human beings suppose that they deserve any special attention from Him? Humans are always so self-centered; why, they even think, usually, that *they* are the chief inhabitants of this planet, and that if a space-ship landed from another planet, it would be the human beings with whom the aliens would communicate, and not the ants or the bees or the microbes.

Maybe all this searching for an answer in the realm of matter is on the wrong track. What is the relationship of God to our universe?

The Jewish philosopher Baruch Spinoza (1632-1677) believed that every part of the universe was inexorably determined by law, and thus, that every single thing follows its course by logical necessity. He did not believe there was any such thing as an accident. According to his system, it was therefore logically impossible for anything to be better than it already was, and if a thing seemed to be bad or evil, that was merely due to the fact that we are not in a position to understand the infinite perfection of the entire universe in its totality. He believed our notions of good and evil are simply subjective assessments of whether or not we considered a thing to be for our own benefit.[50]

---

[50]See discussion on Spinoza in *Evil and the God of Love,* J.Hick, Macmillan, 1966.

Spinoza argued that this subjectivity is misplaced; it is not true that everything is made just for our benefit. In order for a universe to be perfect, it would have to include a full range of experiences and beings, the lower as well as the higher; any universe that did not contain the full range would be less perfect than one that did. Therefore, he argued, there must be room for the sinner as well as the saint.

Evolutionists discount the idea of humanity's falling from an original state of perfection into sin. The whole theory of evolution is based on the gradual progress of living things through countless changing forms in a steady upward trend toward complexity. According to this reasoning, maybe our moral awareness is no more than a part of that gradual progress, from rudimentary self-consciousness to a caring concern for the whole of humanity. Dogs and cats care for their families, but they do not regard dogs' dying of starvation as an evil. The awareness that something could be thought of as evil has developed somewhere along the road as humans ceased to be just animals.

So far, all the theories under consideration have been based on the material universe as we know it. But what about the spiritual universe? Maybe it doesn't matter that much if we suffer pain or evil in this world of ours, because we will be compensated in the world to come for our suffering. The evil and the good — both will receive from the infinite justice of God the recompense of what they earned .

If human beings are to be permitted to have free will, there has to exist the possibility of a range of choices, and inevitably some of the things we choose to do will be less good than others. Some of our choices will cause a great deal of pain and suffering to others; some will produce hatred, envy, greed, malice, fear, despair, contempt, pride, cruelty, cowardice, avarice and lust!

We have been speaking of evil as if we knew what it was. But what kinds of things are evil? It seems that there are two main sorts of evil, physical and moral. 'Physical evil' is suffering which arises from natural causes such as droughts, floods, earthquakes, diseases, and so on, and we can perhaps concede that although these may be unfortunate for the human beings affected by them, they are totally locked into the working-out of the natural law of cause-and-effect.

The many people who claim to feel a religious awareness

through the beauties of nature — things like the blossoms of spring and glorious sunsets — are often taking rather a sentimental and one-sided view, for nature is also 'red in tooth and claw,' and is not really calm or gentle or peaceful at all. So often, we exist *in spite of* nature. Nature cares nothing for those it wipes out. There is there no element of 'justice' in natural disasters. A landslide can just as well fall on masses of innocent children as on one villain.

Nature is governed by rules which do not change to suit our needs or convenience. And the same rules apply when we humans act, for we are part of nature too. If we bomb people with napalm, they are burned. Bullets kill, drunken driving kills, carelessness in industry and in the home kills.

Are these things really God's fault? I mean, isn't it rather unfair and unreasonable to expect God to break the laws of nature on our behalf? If we ran for the bus and missed it, and then prayed to God to make the bus come back for our benefit, we would have started a chain reaction in which the bus would actually travel backward and not forward, and never reach its destination! If we were sitting under a falling rock and God kindly altered the laws of gravity on our behalf so that we would not be crushed, it might result in countless millions of beings' shooting off to their doom in space. And then, whose petition would God, if He chose to do so at all, respond to — yours, mine, someone else's? But what if each of us were praying for a different thing, one which would go counter to the requests of the other supplicants?

The three monotheistic faiths, Judaism, Christianity, and Islam, teach (and it seems a pretty reasonable demand anyway) that it's our business to live within the laws of nature and use them as best we can for the benefit of humanity and the planet. If we pollute our atmosphere, or destroy our oxygen-producing rainforests, or wipe out endangered species, or eliminate wild plants whose medicinal properties might prove to be the very things we need as cures or antidotes, or eradicate our protective ozone layer, the responsibility is surely ours. How then can we blame God?

> Mischief has appeared on land and sea because of (the corruption) wrought by the hands of men (surah 30:41).

But what about moral evil? Moral evil is the result of our own actions — not the bad things that we do through ignorance, but deliberately unkind and malicious deeds; it arises through intentional negligence, selfishness, hatred and spite. As we have seen, spiritual evolution can only take place if there is free will, and for free will to exist there has to be the possibility of making wrong or immoral choices, or doing some things that are less good than others. This must mean, inevitably, that in order to be free, we are bound to live in an environment full of dangers and challenges, an environment in which the results of our own free choices can damage ourselves and others.

In this century, people have had to live with the awful knowledge that they can completely destroy their entire environment and their whole species; the free will exercised by a single man with his finger on a button could wipe out the whole of life as we know it. It is the existence of human free will that allows individuals to be in such a position of authority. It was *our* tax money that paid the wages of the scientists who invented the bombs, *our* votes (or our negligence) that put the various tyrants in power over us.

In the story of Adam and Eve, the first human couple was created perfect, but like all subsequent humans, they were endowed with free will. They chose to disobey God's command — that is, to sin. Before eating the forbidden fruit, Adam was neither good nor evil; in fact, he was not a moral being at all, since he had never exercised his freedom of choice. But after eating, along with his knowledge came responsibility.

This does not answer the criticism that if God had not created a special tree, told Adam that if he ate of its fruit he would suffer, and then given him (a) the choice of whether or not to eat from it, and (b) the opportunity to do so, Adam would not have gotten himself into difficulties and upset his Maker.

If God were to remove the evil choices open to us, we could not justifiably be called 'good' at all, but would simply be mindless automatons and not free souls. Most of us would not be interested in that sort of existence. Could a life totally devoid of freedom be fulfilling in any way, let alone the conceived will of God for us?

CHAPTER SIXTEEN

FATE AND FREE WILL

We have noticed that everything in the universe is governed by the laws of cause and effect. This knowledge is the whole basis of science. If the universe did not follow laws, then we would never be able to reason things out, make predictions, and observe whether our theories were true or not. Nobody seriously doubts the statement that the principle of causation rules the whole of the realm of matter.

However, when we consider a human being, we begin to wonder whether we are dealing solely with the realm of matter, or whether there might not be something else involved as well. Is a human individual just a clever machine that must inevitably follow these natural laws, or is there another aspect—call it Mind or Soul—which is not necessarily obliged to be a 'prisoner' of those laws but might perhaps control them in order to mold that individual's own destiny?

Suppose we could acquire all the information about a person, all the bits of his parents' genetic patterns that he had inherited, all the influences acting on him through his background and education. Could we then predict exactly how he would behave in any given situation? Could we work out what he would do next in a crisis? Could we predict from such information how the adult character of a child would develop?

One who thinks such prediction is possible is termed a determinist. Those who would go even further than this and claim that all future events are already mapped out, and that nothing you could do in your life could alter your fate at all, are known as fatalists. They maintain that human activity is not free at all, but pre-

determined by all sorts of rules and motives acting on the will, and
that anything we 'choose' to do is predetermined by the sort of
persons we are.

The word 'fate' comes from the Latin '*fatum*,' meaning 'what
has been spoken.' It presupposes some Entity which is in control, a Divine Mind or Order in the universe, the plan of which
cannot be altered once it has been formalized. Once a thing has
been 'spoken' or 'written,' there is no escaping it; it must come
to pass.

Fatalists do not necessarily think of this Entity as a personalized being or a God; many simply accept that the universe is governed by the abstract framework of the laws of nature, without any
divine originator. It is the overall law itself which can never be
altered or avoided, but each happening or observed phenomenon
is the direct result of predetermined causes that have acted upon
it. The plan, therefore, is inexorable and totally unavoidable.

Hence, fatalists believe that if one could be given full knowledge of all the facts and influences that were going to bear upon
an individual's life, the details of that life could be inexorably predicted, even the time and condition of that individual's ultimate
demise. All events are really results following causes which are
laws fixed in advance, and human beings are powerless to change
things, no matter how much they may desire or attempt to do so.

Other fatalists have a more personalized idea of the Divine
Force and turn the whole process around. They take the point of
view that God is Omniscient and therefore knows everything concerning everyone's past, present and future simultaneously, and
that from the moment of a soul's conception or implantation in a
body, He knows the exact moment when it will leave it. In other
words, if the moment of your death has been fixed at 3:30 p.m. on
a particular day, then, even though you may decide to stay in bed
and not risk going out, the ceiling will cave in on you or you will
have a fatal heart attack or some such thing, and you will not be
able to escape your moment.

The problem of whether or not we have free will is therefore
twofold, based on the prior questions of whether or not it is true
that God exists and has absolute knowledge of everything, and
whether or not there is some part of a human being which is
immaterial and not subject to the laws of nature.

Obviously, if there really is a God, He should know everything.

If He is outside time, then while we are experiencing our present, He will know what our future will be. If He does know this, then what we are going to do in the future must, in some mysterious fashion outside our time, be predetermined and fixed. Therefore it seems that we are *not* actually free.

Thinkers from the earliest of times have struggled with this problem of whether human beings have free will or are bound by fate. Socrates, for example, argued that it was nothing more than ignorance that made human beings the playthings of fate, and that education and knowledge would bring them freedom. Plotinus (24-270 C.E.) emphasized the difference between that which was spiritual and that which was governed by the laws of matter. He believed that the souls of human beings were free, but as soon as these immaterial souls entered material bodies, they became subject to physical laws.

Fatalism has molded the belief and outlook of countless millions of believers, although members of the different faiths tend to have somewhat divergent perspectives. Some people accept the notion of 'fortune'—that their actions can be guided by the tossing of a coin or some other such method. Millions of people believe that their future is predetermined by the movement and position of the stars. A recent poll in the United States revealed that around sixty percent of the young people surveyed believed in astrology, and astrology is a key aspect of religion in China and Japan.

Hindus and Buddhists believe in *karma*, claiming that there are eternal laws of cause and effect that govern the lives of all people, and relying on the idea of reincarnation to provide answers for some of the problems raised. The doctrine of reincarnation puts forward belief in a multiplicity of lives in this world, a process of death and rebirth, in which the events and conditions of a person's present life are the direct result of his or her actions in a previous incarnation. Thus, some 'inexplicable' tragedies that appear to nullify the idea that God is gracious and kind are explained in terms of just punishment for something a person did in a previous life, and the sense of eternal justice is restored.

Jews, Christians and Muslims, on the other hand, reject the notion that human souls pass through long chains of lifetimes in various bodily forms. Instead, they believe that all human beings have but one lifetime here on earth, which, they generally agree, is in some way a test or trial that determines their eternal fates in the life hereafter.

Obviously, there is a problem here. If human beings face judgement concerning their earthly lives, then they must be able to freely exercise a genuine and meaningful morality while on earth. This is particularly vital if human beings only get one chance at it—that is, are not reincarnated. In other words, if a God, karma, or anything else, is to attempt to make any sort of judgement on us, there has to be the possibility of our making genuine choices based on our own value judgements. Otherwise, judgement does not apply; if a person is not free to make a choice, then he or she cannot be held responsible for pursuing any course of action.

Believers in God insist that, while it may indeed be true that our personalities do depend to a great extent on our inherited characteristics — the physical bodies we have been given and our environment, particularly in our early years — we are not programmed robots. Not everyone reacts in the same way to a given situation; some of us are much more unselfish, generous, forgiving, helpful and able to cope than others. But we don't *have* to be. Although we are born with the ability to recognize and practice basic goodness, it is entirely up to us whether or not we use those abilities. If we see an old lady struggling up the road, carrying heavy parcels, we can *choose* whether to go to help her, knock her down and steal her parcels, ignore her, or shout rude epithets at her and run away.

This leads on to an interesting thought. We can entertain ourselves by guessing what any particular individual might do to the old lady. But we all have a feeling of 'ought'; we think we know what course of action the good person, the religious person, the person of conscience, ought to take. Whenever we say that a person *ought* to do something, we assume that the person is actually free and able to do it. Kant (1724-1804) clearly realized this when he insisted that human freedom was a moral necessity, for without it we cannot be considered responsible for the things we do. It is quite pointless to say that someone ought to help his sick mother, for example, if that person is locked up in jail or unconscious or living in a distant country. 'Ought' implies 'can'. However, say the fatalists, if God knows everything, then He must know in advance what any person is going to do at any time. And since actions are thus foreknown, they must be predestined. So where is the freedom of choice?[51]

Against the notion of inevitable fate, however, the sacred scriptures of Judaism, Christianity and Islam maintain that people *can* influence what lies in store for them in the future. They are able to do this because aspects of their promised futures are conditional.

The key to understanding human free will lies in distinguishing between the brain and the mind or soul—whether these are to be identified as a single entity or as two separate and distinct ones. The brain is a physical thing, part of the world of matter and subject to all its conditions; the mind and soul are not physical or material, but are able to exert the influence of will over the body. If human beings possess the freedom to choose various courses of action, the part that makes the choices is the mind, and God does not control anyone's mind by force.

Now, if God can do anything He wants, then it would obviously be perfectly possible for Him to control our minds and our choices. This is a matter that is within the capabilities of human beings themselves, and it would be only too easy for God. However, the very fact that He allows people to choose *not* to believe in Him and *not* to do what He wants, demonstrates conclusively that God does not robotize peoples' minds.

Therefore, whereas we have to accept that nothing can happen without the knowledge of God, who knows the present, past and future of all created beings, and whereas whether we are or are not going to obey or disobey Him is also known to Him, it nevertheless does not affect our freedom to make choices. We humans do not know what our destiny is, and therefore, whenever we choose what particular course we will take, we cannot be influenced by prior knowledge.

Each of the prophets, including Abraham, Moses, Jesus and Muhammad, taught that what people chose to do with respect to belief in God and obedience to His will makes a very great difference in the final outcome of their affairs. Simply because human beings have conscious souls, they have a tremendous ability to love and be kind, or to hate and be destructive. This means that

---

[51]For a discussion on Kant, see *The Critique of Pure Reason*, I. Kant, trans. J.M.D. Meiklejohn, Chicago, 1955. Also in the *Philosophy of Religion*, H.D. Lewis, 1965, pp. 192.

although they may have all been born with souls of equal worth, they do not remain equal. Due to their inherent capability of bearing responsibility, the spiritual faculties of human beings raise them up above the level of the animal kingdom, although individuals, of course, behave so badly that they in fact sink below the level of animals.

The sacred scriptures of all three of the monotheistic faiths — Judaism, Christianity and Islam—insist that God sent guidance to mankind from the beginning of the human race. They hold that human free will is a vital and decisive factor in our ultimate destinies, and is, in fact, the precise reason why God chose messengers, revealing Himself to them. What, it may be asked, was the main point of such revelations? To this the monotheistic faiths unanimously reply, 'Guidance, so individuals may be able to make the right choices and decisions to guide the actions of their lives.' If it had been impossible to do this because our actions and ultimate destinies were all predetermined, then there would have been no point whatsoever in such messengers and revelations.

According to Islam, if any part of humanity did not have the opportunity to hear the revealed words of God and His warnings, they would still be in a state of innocence, or ignorance, for which they could hardly be blamed. If it is humanity's duty to love and serve God and submit to His will, then obviously they have to be given the opportunity to know what that will is. Therefore the necessity of revelation is part and parcel of the notion of God's justice and mercy toward us.

Muslims believe that God revealed Himself to those whom He chose and trained, individuals who possessed the spirituality to understand. The messengers did not choose to do this work; on the contrary, God chose them, much to the surprise and reluctance of some of them. If it were impossible for people to choose to do God's will because their destinies were already immovably fixed, not only would God be unfair instead of just, but there would also seem to be very little point in their making any attempt to live good lives. One of the very real dangers of fatalism is the despair and helplessness such an attitude engenders. Whether or not an individual actually is helpless, if he or she *feels* helpless, that induces a passivity which becomes superstitious and does not promote the development of character and inner strength. On the contrary, it often leads to defeatism, hindering the individual from making any effort to improve either his lot or the lot of those around him.

Those who believe absolutely in fate therefore run into the same problem as did the Greek philosopher Zeno of Citium, who lived in the third century B.C.E. He caught his slave stealing and proposed to beat him for it, but the slave retorted that he had no right to do so, since it was fated that he should steal.

If criminals were simply living out their destinies, then the responsibility for that would rest not with those poor humans, but with the one who fixed their actions, God Himself. In terms of God as First Cause, which we have been considering, this would also logically mean that God is the First Cause of all the wickedness, violence, oppression and evil ever committed by human beings, a concept that totally contradicts the understanding of God which was presented by the prophets.

The whole ethos of the sacred scriptures of the monotheistic tradition is that there *are* alternative destinies for us, and that it is up to us to try to live in such a way that God may be pleased with us and admit us to His exalted Divine Presence in Paradise. Basically the message is the same: keep to God's path and live a life of righteousness, so that God may accept you, your earthly life will be meaningful and blessed, and your eternal life will be joyful and not anguished.

We must consider the possibility that God does indeed know everything, but that, at the same time, He leaves with us the choice of different courses of action. He must be able to see all the possible outcomes of whatever courses of action we choose, but in His Wisdom leave us free to make those choices.[52]

---

[52]See *Islam Between East* and *West*, Alija Ali Izetbegovic, American Trust publications, 1993, pp. 114-115: 'The inner span of man is huge, almost infinite. He is capable of the most abominable crimes and the most noble sacrifices. The greatness of man is not primarily in the doing of good deeds but in his ability to choose. Everyone who reduces or limits this choice debases man. Good does not exist beyond one's will, nor can it be imposed by force. There is no force in faith.' See also Qur'an 2:256.

CHAPTER SEVENTEEN

TESTING IT OUT

The business of coping with evil is the most taxing of subjects for those who want to live in submission to God's will. Is evil something that should be recognized as an enemy and fought against? Or is it something that should be accepted as just another manifestation of God's inscrutable plan and order for us, which we do not as yet understand?

Any believer who accepts the notion that every aspect of the universe, with all its laws and life forms, is decreed by God's will in keeping with His divine plan, must also accept in his or her heart the inexorable logic that ultimately God is indeed responsible for all that happens in that universe, even the things that seem to us to be tragedies.

According to the view of Islam, all things proceed from God's divine omnipotence, mercy and justice. Mercy is described in the Qur'an as the fundamental attribute of God, and it 'extends to all things' (surah 7:156). The creation of the universe, life, and humanity — these are manifestations of His infinite mercy:

> It is out of His mercy that He has made for you (both) night and day — that you may rest in the one, and (actively) seek of His grace (in the other) — and in order that you may be grateful (surah 28:73).

> It is He Who brought you forth from the wombs of your mothers when you knew nothing; and He gave you hearing and sight and intelligence and affection that you may give thanks (to Him) (surah 16:78).

> And He has subjected to you, as from Him, all that is
> in the heavens and on earth: behold, in that are signs
> indeed for those who reflect (surah 45:13).

God's greatest gift to humanity, however, is the faculty of reasoning and a free will. This freedom of action carries with it a
guarantee that all people shall have the opportunity to exercise
their free will.

> Verily We created man from a drop of mingled sperm,
> in order to try him: so We gave him (the gifts) of hearing
> and sight. We showed him the Way: whether he be grate-
> ful or ungrateful (rests on his will) (surah 76:2-3).

Whenever people misuse their powers, or stray from the
explicit Will of their Creator as it is expressed in the guidance
revealed to His prophets, they are in conflict with the rest of the
creation that is subject to His Will. This abuse of free will on the
part of human beings is the cause of all mischief, misery and corruption. The only way to remove this kind of moral evil from life
is to take away freedom of choice and action, which is nothing
short of depriving humanity of the very *raison d'etre* of their moral
existence.

Furthermore, as to the apparent evil in the physical world,
such as hurricanes, earthquakes, and other natural disasters, our
knowledge is so limited that we cannot comprehend the overall
picture, nor do we understand the purpose behind various happenings and events. But we believe in the essential goodness,
mercy, and beneficence of God, and place our trust in Him:

> Say: He is (God) Most Gracious: we have believed in
> Him, and in Him have we put our trust: so, soon will you
> know which (of us) it is that is in manifest error (surah
> 67:29).

The correct response to God's will, therefore, when it mani-
fests itself in ways which humans find hard to bear, is what the
Muslims call *sabr*, or fortitude. This is the kind of unwavering
steadfastness shown by one who truly believes that, no matter what
happens in life, no matter how bad things may appear to be, God

knows Best, He is Most Gracious and All-Powerful, and that under even the worst of circumstances we are put through, for test and trial, lies God's infinite mercy and beneficence. All these tests and tribulations, adversity and also prosperity, are but means to bring out the best within us and to develop our moral and spiritual potential. Our success and achievement depends on our moral attitude and behavior in various situations. The Prophet (peace be upon him) said:

> Strange are the ways of believers, for there is good in their every affair; and this is not the case with anyone else except believers, for if they have an occasion to feel delight, they thank (God); thus there is a good for them in it. And if they get into trouble and show resignation (and endure it patiently), there is also a good for them in it (Muslim).

Faith in the wisdom of God's decrees and in His absolute control over all things impels Muslims to exercise self-restraint and prevents their jumping to the conclusion that when something happens to an individual that appears to be evil, it really *is* evil. When things go wrong, when tragedies strike, all is not lost; since we may not be aware of the reason for a calamity, we humbly accept that there *is* a reason, a wisdom, and that it is ultimately for our own good, provided we bear to it the correct moral attitude and behavior. Our duty, whatever the situation, is to obey our Lord and do His will, leaving the outcome to Him and praying that it may ultimately be a source of good for us—this is the Islamic way.

Evil stands for all that is contrary to God's will: rebellion and hostility to His law and guidance. Just as belief in God stands for love of God and of all the goodness that flows from Him, abhorrence of evil is also a natural consequence of such a belief. Thus a belief in one is consequent upon the rejection of the other:

> Those who believe fight in the cause of Allah, and those who reject faith fight in the cause of evil (surah 4:76).

Striving, or *jihad* against evil, is thus an extension of our effort to be good. In Islam, 'enjoining what is good' and 'forbidding what is evil' go hand in hand. To be alert to recognize all the forms of evil and immorality around us, and to do one's best to thwart them, is the true significance of the word *jihad* (striving), a prime duty of every Muslim, as the following *hadiths* or sayings of the Prophet demonstrate:

> By Him in whose hand is my soul, you must enjoin what is right and forbid what is wrong, prevent the wrong-doers, bring them into conformity with what is right...or Allah will join your hearts together and curse you as He cursed them (Tirmidhi and Abu Dawud).

> Those among you who see something abominable should rectify it with their hands; if they do not have enough strength to do that, then they should do so with their tongues; and if they do not have the strength enough for that, then they should at least (detest it) in their hearts, and that is weakest of faith (Muslim).

Islam recognizes the right of individuals to profess and follow the faith of their choice. The Qur'an says:

> Let there be no compulsion in religion: truth stands out clear from error: whoever rejects evil and believes in God has grasped the most trustworthy handhold that never breaks (surah 2:256).

There is therefore no question of imposing Islamic beliefs or morality on non-Muslims by force. Those who profess Islam and willingly accept its discipline are, however, expected to abide by its discipline and rules of life.

The Qur'an sets forth quite specific teachings about evil that put certain conclusions beyond the range of doubt for the Muslim. For a start, in relation to Adam and Eve, it teaches that the first human beings were a unique creation, and that at the root of all the world's evil lies the misuse of the free will that God has given to humans. Both Adam and Eve, the Qur'an says, were deceived by Satan and disobeyed God. Later they repented and were forgiven, no stigma of sin being left attached to them or their future generations. This demonstrated that humans are weak and need God's support, help, and guidance to follow the right path. For that purpose, God promised to guide and support humanity by raising among them His prophets and giving them guidance.

To follow God's guidance, however, rests on human choice and willingness. The Qur'an tells us that people have been given an innate knowledge of good and evil:

> Consider the human self, and how it is formed in accordance to what it is meant to be, and how it is imbued with moral failings as well as with consciousness of God (surah 91:7-8).

Likewise God gave humans the faculty of reason and the faculties of hearing and sight, and then showed them the right path, but He left the choice to them: if they choose to follow the right path, God guides them and helps them, but if they decide to go the other way, God leaves them alone and gives them the opportunity to follow the paths of their choice:

> Thus, as for those who give [to others] and are conscious of God, and believe in the truth of the ultimate good — for them shall We make easy the path toward [ultimate] ease. But as for those who are greedy misers, and think that they are self-sufficient, and call the ultimate good a lie — for them shall We make easy the path toward hardship (surah 92:5-10).

Skeptical materialists, who feel that modern science has explained away everything supernatural, are always scornful of the fact that the Bible and the Qur'an emphasize belief in the unseen. Even believers who would also like to seem scientifically 'respectable' are frankly embarrassed by it. They would definitely prefer that anything which does not fit in with modern materialism not be there at all.[53]

-----

[53]The Tubingen school of theology in Germany, for example, made it its crusade to have biblical scholars 'demythologize' their texts. Perhaps the most influential of these scholars was Rudolf Bultmann, in

According to the Qur'an, God has created several orders of beings other than humans — beings that we cannot normally see. Of these, angels belong to the highest order of beings and are employed by God in the execution of various of His commands. Angels do not have free will but do exactly what God tells them: '(The angels) flinch not (from executing) the commands they receive from God, but do (precisely) what they are commanded' (surah 66:6). Besides angels there also exist the jinn, who, like humans, enjoy freedom of choice. The jinn who choose evil are led by Satan, about whom the Qur'an says: 'He was one of the Jinn, and he broke the command of his Lord' (surah 18:50) when he refused to bow before Adam on account of arrogance and envy. In his arrogance, he challenged God that he would do his best to prove that Adam and his children did not deserve the great honor he had bestowed upon them:

> Behold We said to the angels: 'Bow down unto Adam.' They bowed down, except Satan: He said: 'See this (one) whom You have honored above me! If You will but give me respite until the Day of Judgement, I will surely bring his children under my sway—all but a few!' (surah 17:61-62)

God gave Satan the respite he asked for, saying:

> Go your way;...(and) lead to destruction those whom you can among them, with your (seductive) voice, make

---

whose many books it was always taken for granted that if a narrative included a 'mythological' element that was not supported by modern science, such as the miracles of Jesus, it could be safely concluded that it was false. (See *Kerygma and Myth*, SPCK, 1953, ed. Hans Werner Bartsch (contributions by Bulkmann and others).

The doctrine of the Virgin Birth of Jesus was one of the earliest doctrines to need 'demythologizing,' with the consequent undermining of the Trinitarian atonement theology. Various church leaders in the UK, notable among them the famous Bishop David Jenkins of Durham, felt they were even able to hold high church office while doubting the most fundamental of Christian beliefs. Believing inexorably in the materialistic 'truths' of science, they feel it is their duty to reinterpret all the scriptures of the more 'gullible' past in a way that explains the supernatural in terms of myth and symbol, rather than as literal truth.

assaults on them with your cavalry and your infantry;
mutually share with them wealth and children; and make
promises to them; but Satan promises them nothing but
deceit. As for My (sincere) servants, no authority shall you
have over them (surah 17:63-65).

Thus, according to the Qur'an, the origin of evil is divergence
from the stated will of God, beginning with the devil's animosity
toward humans when they were first created. God honored the
first man, Adam, and made him His vicegerent on earth. But
Satan rebelled against the divine command and challenged God
that man did not truly deserve the high position given to him.
Since that time, Satan has done his best to lead people away from
God, but he has no power to actually force anyone to take an evil
course. So long as humans stand firm in their faith, they have
nothing to fear from Satan and his allies, for their powers are limited and can be overcome with the help of God,[54] whose forgiveness is always readily available to those who are sorry for their mis-
takes and ask His forgiveness. According to a hadith, the Prophet
said:

Truly, the devil said: 'By Your honor, O Lord, I shall
not cease to misguide Your servants as long as life remains
in their bodies.' The Almighty and Glorious Lord said:
'By My Honor, Greatness, and Exalted rank, I shall not
cease to forgive them as long as they seek forgiveness of
Me' (Ahmad).

If one pauses to consider, in the light of divine revelation, the
reason for human life, it becomes clear that it is not just to wander
about aimlessly enjoying oneself and avoiding pain and evil as best
one can, but it is for a higher purpose. The privileged position
that we occupy in this life entails responsibilities. If life has any
purpose behind it, then we must be concerned with how to
achieve that purpose and avoid failure and futility. The Qur'an
says:

---

[54] The Qur'an actually mentions (in surah 72) that some jinn, who
had heard the words of a revelation to the Prophet, accepted them and
became Muslims.

> Did you then think that We had created you in jest,
> and that you would not be brought back to Us (for
> account)? (surah 75:36).

Difficult circumstances or traumatic events are meant to test
our real mettle, bringing out the best in us by challenging our
consciences and energies. Patience in the face of difficulties and
hardships, and gratitude in the case of good fortune, is good for a
person because, at the end of it, he or she is promised great
reward and an eternal abode of sublime serenity and joy — Paradise. The prophet Muhammad said: 'Allah's merchandise is
dear. Allah's merchandise is Paradise' (Tirmidhi). Only through
striving in the cause of Allah alone can one achieve this supreme
success:

> God has purchased of the believers their persons and
> their goods; for theirs (in return) is the Garden (of Par-
> adise) (surah 2:155-156).

The person who has such trust in God possesses a calmness, a
steadfastness that is part of his or her armor against the cruelties
of life. And when death occurs, faith is not lost nor confidence
shaken, for death is part of the scheme of things, and the Muslim's
attitude toward death is that everyone must sooner or later experience it. Therefore, what Muslims are worried about is not death
itself, but how best to utilize the time they have at their disposal
before its advent.

> And spend something (in charity) out of the sub-
> stance which We have bestowed on you, before death
> should come to any of you and you should say, 'O my
> Lord! Why did you not give me respite for a little while? I
> should then have given (generously) in charity, and I
> should have been of the doers of good!' But to no soul
> will God grant respite when the time appointed (for it)
> has come (surah 63:10-11).

Death in itself is not a calamity that befalls humans; it is rather
the moving on of the human soul to a higher level of existence,
which we, with our limited physical faculties, cannot perceive. So

although believers are just as sad as anyone else to lose their loved ones, their attitude is one of trustful acceptance and reliance on the mercy of God.

Why should God want to test us? Well, it is from these tests that we may grow out of weakness and selfishness and become strong, faithful individuals — ones who warrant repayment and reward for their patience and striving.

God allows evil to exist alongside good for the same purpose: to test mankind and provide them with the opportunity to follow evil or good, as they so choose. We have the freedom to decide whether or not *we* will be evil, and we have to decide what to do about people who are. We can choose whether to gratify the desires of our own lower selves, or to put God before our desire for self-gratification.

Accordingly, we have to work out how to react toward wrong-doing and evil. If a person does something wrong to another, there are three ways in which evil can win a victory, and only two in which it can be defeated. We can retaliate in anger, nurse a grudge, or take it out on someone else. In each of these cases, the evil is kept going and passed along. But evil is defeated if the injured person is generous enough to 'take the coin out of use,'— that is, to forgive the person who has caused the offense and stop the chain of evil from going any further. The Qur'an says:

> Nor can goodness and evil be equal. Repel evil with that which is better: then will the one between whom and you was hatred become as it were your friend and intimate (surah 41:34).

There are cases of unmitigated and unrepentant evil, however, in which persons or groups will not desist from wrongdoing and oppression, no matter how much kindness and forgiveness is offered them. In that case, according to Islam, the injured party is mandated to repel evil by force, not out of a desire for revenge, but in order to preserve justice and the rights of the oppressed. In regard to such cases, the Qur'an says:

> If God did not check one set of people by means of another, the earth would indeed be full of corruption (surah 2:251).

The idea of stopping evil by force may be upsetting to those
bred on pacifism, but to think that all evil can be turned away by
good is naive and unsupported by history. However, God is merciful and loves mercy, and the use of force is thus reserved as the last
resort. The Qur'an emphasizes that when feasible, forgiveness is
the better way:

> It is part of the mercy of God that you should deal
> gently with those (who have offended you, or who have
> sinned). If you were severe with them, or harsh-hearted,
> they would have broken away from you. So pass over (their
> faults), and ask for forgiveness for them (surah 3:159).

> O My servants, who have transgressed against their
> souls! Do not despair of the mercy of God; for God for-
> gives all sins; He is Oft-Forgiving, Most Merciful. (surah
> 39:53).

It is the love of God which unblocks the coldness, bitterness,
the ache of bereavement, the pain of loneliness and rejection, the
resentment of our ill-treatment by others. Maybe life is given to us
specifically so that we can learn how to believe, love God, and love
our fellow human-beings and treat them with compassion. The
Prophet said: 'You cannot believe until you love one another'
(Muslim). In another hadith he said: 'God, the Compassionate
One, has mercy on those who are merciful. If you show mercy to
those who are on earth, He Who is in the heaven will show mercy
to you' (Abu Dawud).

Practical people maintain that genuine morality requires stan-
dards that are universally acceptable. It would seem to be universally acceptable, for example, that we should 'do unto others as we
would wish them to do unto us.' The monotheistic religions teach
that it is our duty to love God more than anyone or anything, to
obey His orders as well as we can, and to treat others with kindness
and compassion.

The Muslim strives to take a complete overview of life, the universe and all aspects of reality. Is all this just a meaningless journey from chaos to utter annihilation, or is it the amazing and intricate brilliance of a supreme plan worked out by a divine Mind?
Are we just blobs of atomic bits and pieces, or does it matter that

we are individuals, who can feel love and comprehend and worship? Do we just blunder through our lives from our unchosen
births to our unwanted deaths, or do we live according to some
conscience-driven intelligence that seems guided, and according
to which we suffer and cause suffering when we deviate from it? Is
it all aimless and the result of chance, or are we being tested and
prepared for a future state of being?

We can pass our lives as automatons, like machines, or we can
take the leap of faith and change our entire motivation. Even if
we cannot prove the existence of God, we could start to alter our
lives and behave in such a way *as if* He did exist, as if He *could* see
us, as if He *did* understand all our inner thoughts and motivations,
as if it *did* matter how we reacted to our each and every test, each
waking moment. Then, I suppose, if we were being 'scientific,' we
could compare for ourselves the results of the two ways of living
and form a judgement as to which was the most profitable, the
most comfortable, the most integrating and the most reasonable.

The Muslim has made this leap of faith. And so we come full
circle back to the Muslim *shahada*, the Declaration of Faith:

> *La ilaha illal Lahu wa Muhammadur Rasulullah* (There
> is no deity except God [Allah], and Muhammad is the
> Messenger of God).

There are those who bewail their lot in life and complain that
life on earth is like being flung into the midst of a complicated
technical situation without any manual or map to find one's way
or to cope with it, or control it. For the Muslim there is no such
confusion or lack of direction; it seems so obvious that a just God
would never be so cruel as to leave His beloved servants in such
terrible uncertainty.

In his final sermon, the blessed prophet Muhammad told his
followers: I have left with you two things—the Qur'an and my *Sun-
nah* (his teachings, example, and way of life). Hold fast to these
two, and you will not go astray from the right path (Al-Muwatta).
There is no need to wander about blindly, groping in the darkness
and grasping nothing. The signposts have been placed and are
there for all to find and follow, if only they will open their eyes
and begin to look.

Opening the eyes of the spirit takes a certain courage and a moment of decision. It is as if the world were full of people who would like to swim, and who might be prepared to read all the relevant literature about swimming and practice all sorts of exercises, but they are nervous about getting into the water. Their minds are assailed by all manner of doubts and uncertainties; that is the nature of the human mind. One could sit on the edge of the pool all day long, theorizing about the techniques and benefits of swimming, or even speculating on whether the pool has real existence or is only a figment of the imagination, a hallucination; or one could plunge into it, and find that it is real, and that swimming in it is very invigorating both for the body and soul of the swimmer!

The beginner paddles in the shallows and then gains a little confidence by practicing in the safe confines of the pool. A more experienced swimmer can float like a tiny speck upon the surface of a vast ocean of unimaginable depth and still feel safe and confident in the hands of God.

The moment of realization that maybe it *is* all real is where submission to God begins.   It is not the end of the story by any means, but only the beginning.   What follows from that is a lifetime of becoming familiar with the landmarks of the blessed path to which we have been guided, and then following it to the best of our ability until God allows us to call our work finished and return to Him.

INDEX